WILD
BERRIES & FRUITS
FIELD GUIDE ROCKY MOUNTAIN STATES

by Teresa Marrone

Adventure Publications
Cambridge, Minnesota

ACKNOWLEDGMENTS

Special thanks to Chris and Neil Swanson; Joe Musich; Irene Collins and Bob Schumacher (and Paul Schumacher for the fly-fishing lesson–we'll catch you next time, Andy); Mike Krebill; the U.S. Forest Service Rangers at Rocky Mountain National Park; and to Bruce Bohnenstingl, the world's best photo assistant and berry scout.

Thanks to Al Schneider for his review of the book.

Cover and book design by Jonathan Norberg

Flower anatomy illustration by Julie Martinez

Edited by Brett Ortler

Photo credits by photographer and page number:
Cover photos: Utah serviceberry, mahonia, black raspberry, common false Solomon's seal and rose hips by Teresa Marrone

All photos by Teresa Marrone unless noted.
James M. Andre: 57 (inset) **Bob Bors/University of Saskatchewan:** 237 (top) **Brad Boyle:** 297 (bottom right) **Amy Buthod:** 303 (main) **Ken Cave:** 243 (main) **Michael L. Charters:** 173 **Alfred Cook:** 69 **Paul A. Cornelius:** 185 **Jessie Harris:** 233 (main) **Jason Hollinger:** 277 **Gertrud Konings:** 65 (right inset), 111 (main), 119, 121 **Nick Kurzenko:** 237 (bottom) **Melody Lytle:** 215 **Karen Matsumoto:** 129 (inset) **J. Andrew McDonald:** 243 (inset) **Mike Millar:** 239 **Lorena Babcock Moore:** 285 **Walter Muma:** 259 **Glenn Naylor:** 311 **Paul Noll:** 123 **Bruce J. Patt:** 75, 175, 223, 231 (top, inset), 253 (both), 287 (both) **Don Poggensee:** 83 **Jan Samanek/State Phytosanitary Administration, Bugwood.org:** 207 (both) **Al Schneider:** 89 (top), 113 (main), 183 (bottom), 211, 233 (inset) **Jay W. Sharp:** 297 (bottom left) **Clinton C. Shock:** 279 **Bob Sivinski:** 133 (inset), 149 **James N. Stuart:** 53 **Amber Swanson:** 43 **Kathy Voth:** 33 **Andy and Sally Wasowski:** 127 **Loraine Yeatts:** 57 (main), 297 (top) **Dale A. Zimmerman Herbarium, Western New Mexico University:** 111 (inset), 129 (main), 303 (inset)

10 9 8 7 6 5 4 3 2

Wild Berries & Fruits Field Guide: Rocky Mountain States
Copyright © 2012 by Teresa Marrone
Published by Adventure Publications, an imprint of AdventureKEEN
310 Garfield Street South
Cambridge, Minnesota 55008
(800) 678-7006
www.adventurepublications.net
Printed in China
ISBN 978-1-59193-281-9 (pbk.)

TABLE OF CONTENTS

Introduction

The Berries and Fruits

ABOUT THIS BOOK

Numerous field guides are available to aid in flower identification, but few address the fruiting stage of the plant. Those that do usually add a footnote or a small photo of the fruit. But the fruiting stage is critical to the plant and interesting to observers of nature as well. This book is specifically about that glorious stage in a plant's life when it fulfills its purpose by producing fruits to help it reproduce.

This book is unique as it was written with the forager in mind, and especially for foragers interested in taking home their finds and using them in recipes and in the kitchen. For this reason, this book makes references to *Cooking with Wild Berries & Fruits of the Rocky Mountain States,* a companion cookbook that includes recipes, handy tips, and different uses for many of the edible species found in this book.

In addition to showing edible berries and fruits, this book also identifies those berries and fruits which are inedible—even toxic. This information is critical to anyone who is faced with an unknown plant and wishes to know if its fruit is edible. It's also just plain interesting to see all the fascinating and, often, lovely fruits produced by plants, whether that fruit is edible or not.

Photos in this book focus primarily on the fruits, in all their up-close-and-personal glory. However, plant structure and leaf form are also critical to proper identification. The photos here attempt to show the key identification points of each plant; this information is also covered in the text that accompanies each photo. Features that are key to distinguishing a plant from one with similar appearance are in green type in the text; study these points with particular care when looking at a plant.

Habitat and season are also important when attempting to identify a plant. Both of these are covered in the text. Range maps for each species show approximate locations in the Rocky Mountain states where each plant is likely to be found. Helpful information that allows the reader to compare similar plants provides additional insight that will aid in positive identification. Finally, each plant account includes short notes, which may feature interesting tidbits about the plant, how it has been used for food or medicine, or information on how the plant is used by birds and other wildlife.

Common names of plants are often confusing. People in different areas use different names for the same plant, and, sometimes, the same common name is used for two—or more—very different plants. All plant accounts in this book include the common name usually used by the United States Department of Agriculture, and occasionally another common name. More importantly, the scientific name is listed for each species; this is the most definitive nomenclature of all.

Scientific names are based on a system that was standardized in the 1700s by Swedish botanist Carl Linnaeus, often called "the father of taxonomy." These names are binomial, which means they have two parts: a *genus* (family name) and a *species* (the name given to an individual plant within that family); Latin is generally used, although some names have their origins in Greek. Scientific names are accepted throughout the world, so *Prunus armeniaca* refers to the same plant (apricot, in this case) no matter if the person is in the United States or in the apricot's native country, which is most likely Armenia. The benefit of such a system is obvious; no matter what language two people speak, and no matter what a plant is called in their native tongue, both know what plant is being discussed when the scientific name is used.

THE RANGE MAPS

The maps showing plant ranges are based on information from the United States Department of Agriculture, the United States Geological Survey, and the United States Forest Service, updated with data from The Biota of North America Program (BONAP) and several websites that track invasive plants (see pg. 312 for website addresses). These sources have been supplemented with state-specific surveys from natural-resources agencies, universities and herbariums, as well as the author's personal knowledge and experience.

Range maps are a useful tool, but are not an absolute authority. Plants rarely follow state or county lines, but most plant surveyors do when reporting their data to the USDA or other authorities. Further, some counties have not submitted data or been surveyed, and so do not appear on the lists used by government agencies. The maps in this book are approximations, and it is possible to find a plant in an area not shown on the range map (or, conversely, to be unable to find a plant in an area indicated on the map).

WHAT IS A FRUIT?

Since this book is all about fruit, it's worth discussing exactly what that term means in the context of the book. At its most basic, a fruit is the ripened part of a plant that disperses seeds; this includes things like pea pods, wheat heads and nuts. In everyday usage, however, most of us consider only fleshy, juicy, seed-bearing structures, such as blueberries, watermelon and apples, to be "fruit." The short and fairly non-scientific discussion that follows will provide helpful reference for the discussion of various fruit types discussed later.

Like most living things, plants have male and female parts. Depending on species, they may exist together in one flower as illustrated below, or may grow in distinct male or female flowers. (Sometimes the male and female parts don't look anything like this, as with pine trees; then again, these plants don't produce what we think of as fruit.) The female part of the plant, at the center of the flower, is collectively called the *pistil*. It consists of an ovary, topped with a long style, capped with the stigma. The ovary is a case containing one or more carpels, which are ovule-bearing structures containing one or more ovules, or eggs; typically, several carpels are fused together within the ovary, but in a few cases the carpel is single.

The male part of the plant is collectively called the *stamen*. It consists of the pollen-bearing element called the anther, which is supported by the filament, a thin structure that raises the anther above the base of the flower. (The flower petals are there to attract pollinators, by the way—the plant world's version of the little black dress.)

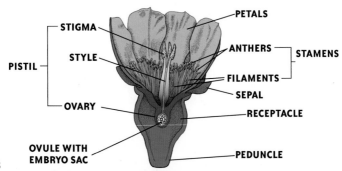

Seeds develop when pollen is introduced into ripe eggs. This service is performed by insects, animals or the wind; regardless of the method, the pollen is deposited onto the sticky stigma, where it germinates, sending the male nuclei down the style to fertilize the eggs. The ovary swells as the seeds mature. The result of all this activity is the fruit—a fleshy structure carrying the fertilized seeds.

Within that narrow definition, there are several types of fruit. Here are short, simple definitions of the types of fruits that are included in this book; please also look at page 19 to see what is *not* included.

BERRIES

A berry is a simple fleshy fruit containing one or more carpels (ovule-bearing structures), each with one or more seeds. The seed coating, or endocarp, is relatively soft. Examples include grapes (pg. 208), gooseberries (pgs. 44, 172, 264–69), currants (pgs. 142, 166, 232, 256, 262, 278, 280) and creeping grape-holly (pg. 224).

Grapes

Gooseberries

Currants

Grape-holly

DRUPES

A drupe, sometimes called a stone fruit, is a simple fleshy fruit with a seed (or on occasion, seeds) contained in a hard pit, or stone. The hard outside of the pit is the endocarp (seed coating). Examples include plums (pgs. 186, 200, 218), three-leaf sumac (pg. 168) and chokecherries (pg. 270).

American wild plum

Three-leaf sumac

Black chokecherry

COMPOUND DRUPES

A compound drupe is a fleshy fruit formed from a single flower, but composed of many drupes, each containing one seed. Compound drupes are typically thought of as "seedy" because they contain so many seeds, each with its own endocarp (seed coating). Examples include red raspberries (pg. 138) and blackberries (pgs. 252, 286).

Red raspberry

Blackberry

Mulberry

MULTIPLE FRUIT

An unusual fruit structure in which a single fruit is formed from multiple flowers that grow closely together in a cluster. Examples of multiple fruits in this book include Osage orange (pg. 50) and mulberries (pg. 198). Figs and pineapples are multiple fruits that don't grow in our region.

POMES

A pome is a pseudocarp, a simple fruit with flesh developed from the receptacle (the end of the flower stalk) rather than the ovary. In pomes, the receptacle surrounds the ovary, and seeds are contained in the carpel, which becomes papery. Examples in this book include wild crabapples (pg. 156), hawthorns (pg. 192), mountain ash (pg. 80) and serviceberries (pg. 216).

Wild crabapple

Hawthorns

Mountain ash

Serviceberry

OTHER TYPES OF FRUIT

Strawberry

Pseudocarps are fruits whose flesh develops from a part other than the ovary. Pomes (pg. 11) are one type. Another is the strawberry (pg. 84); unlike a pome, however, the strawberry carries its seeds on the surface rather than in the center of the fruit.

Wild cucumber

Pepos are berry-like fruits with a very tough rind developed from the receptacle (in most fruits, the skin is developed from the ovary). Wild cucumber (pg. 36) is a pepo that is in this book; others, which are not in this book, are melons and gourds.

Banana yucca

Capsules are dry, non-fleshy fruits that split at maturity to scatter their seeds. Most capsule fruits don't resemble anything we'd think of as fruit and are not included here; however, several, including yucca (pgs. 38, 40) have a large, fleshy capsule that looks like fruit, so they are included.

Common juniper

Cones are fruits that consist of scales (sporophylls) arranged in an overlapping or spiral fashion around a central core; seeds are developed between the scales. Three juniper species (pg. 234, 244) are included in this book because their cones look berry-like.

HOW FRUITS ARE ARRANGED ON THE STEM

Flowers, and the fruits which follow them, may grow singly on a stem, in small bunches of several fruits, or in clusters of many fruits. Locations also vary; they may grow at the ends of branches, along the branches, or in leaf axils. Here are a few common arrangements and locations.

Chokecherry

Some fruits grow in long clusters, like the chokecherries at left; the clusters may hang down or stand upright. Chokecherries produce *racemes*, long clusters of flowers growing on a central stem; each flower has its own stalk, and all stalks are of equal length. The fruits which follow are often described as *racemose*; some sources, including this book, simply say that the fruits grow in racemes, although that term technically describes flowers rather than fruits.

Fruits may also grow in flat-topped or rounded clusters. On some plants, numerous fruit stalks originate from a single point. If the individual fruit stalks are the same length, the cluster will be rounded. On other plants, the individual fruit stalks are of different lengths (or may branch into shorter stalks) so all fruits

Highbush cranberry

are on the same level, producing a flat-topped cluster. The highbush cranberry shown above right has a flat-topped cluster of fruits; the floral arrangement which preceded this is called a *cyme*.

Glossy buckthorn

The *leaf axil* is the point at which the leaf joins the stem; many fruits are attached at the axils. At left are glossy buckthorn fruits growing on short stalks from the leaf axils.

Fruits may also grow at the end of a branch, or at the end of the plant's main stem. At right is a long cluster of common

Common false Solomon's seal

false Solomon's seal fruits growing at the end of the main stem of the plant.

LEAF FORM AND ARRANGEMENT

Leaves are one of the most important features to consider when attempting to identify a plant. Their shape, the way they attach to the plant, characteristics of the edge, and, of course, size and color must all be considered. Botanists use many terms to describe these things in exacting detail; this book does not reach so far, using terms geared to the layperson. Here is a brief overview of some of these terms.

Honeysuckle

Form and arrangement are the first characteristics to look at. The leaves of this honeysuckle are *simple*—a single leaf blade is attached to the stem of the plant. The leaf is narrowly oval, with a rounded base and pointed tip. Looking closer, we see that the leaf has a short *petiole*—the stemlet that attaches the leaf to the stem. The leaf is attached *oppositely*—directly across the stem from another leaf. Its edge is *smooth*, not jagged or toothy. It is deep green and glossy above. The *midrib*—the long line that divides the leaf in two—is pale.

Gooseberry

Although the gooseberry leaves at left are also called simple, there's a lot more going on. They are *lobed*, meaning that each leaf, although whole and undivided, has several distinct sections, rather like a maple leaf. The petiole (stemlet) is much longer than that of the honeysuckle above. The leaves are arranged *alternately* on the stem, with some distance between the points where each leaf attaches to the stem. Leaf veins are noticeable but not prominent, and the midvein does not stand out as on the honeysuckle leaf. Leaf color is medium green above, and the surface is somewhat *rough*; leaf edges have *rounded teeth*, and the base is broad.

Raspberry

Compound leaves look like a small stem with numerous leaves; the entire grouping is called a *blade*. Individual leaves on each blade are called *leaflets*. The blade is a true leaf, with a bud at its base; leaflets don't have buds. This raspberry has three-part compound leaves—each blade has three leaflets, which have *sharply toothed edges*. Compound leaves can have a dozen or more leaflets on each blade. If they are arranged in a row along the blade stem, the blade is said to be *pinnately compound*; see mountain ash on pg. 80 for an example.

Some compound leaves are even more complicated, consisting of several compound leaves attached to the blade stem. The red baneberry pictured at right has *doubly compound* leaves: the blade has three compound leaves, each with five to seven leaflets. This plant has three doubly compound leaves: the one at the top, which also is bearing the fruiting stalk, and the two that are going off to the sides near the bottom of the photo.

Red baneberry

Woodbine

The final type of compound leaf is called *palmately compound*. As shown by the leaves of this woodbine, the leaflets all radiate from a central point, rather than growing on a blade stem.

Note that characteristics of the individual leaves shown here, other than leaf form, are not always as shown. For example, a simple leaf can have a long or short petiole (or no petiole); its edges may be pointed or smooth, and it may grow alternately.

LEAF ATTACHMENT

The previous pages showed some examples of leaf attachment; this page gives additional examples of those, as well as a few others that were not shown. Note that the text discusses the attachment of a leaf to the stem, but the same attachment styles could also apply to the attachment of a leaflet to a blade stem (on a compound leaf).

Golden currant

Many leaves are attached to the stem by a *petiole*, which can be defined as a leaf stemlet. Petioles can be long or short, smooth or hairy, round or flattened, and any color found in nature. The petioles on the golden currant leaves shown at left are long, smooth and greenish.

Some leaves are *sessile*—they attach directly to the stem. The false Solomon's seal shown below left is an example of this. *Perfoliate* leaves, like those of the large-flowered bellwort shown below right, have a base that extends slightly beyond the stem, giving the impression that the stem is growing up through the leaf.

False Solomon's seal

Large-flowered bellwort

Clasping leaves have no petiole (stemlet); the base of the leaf clasps, or slightly surrounds, the stem, but does not extend beyond it. Smooth Solomon's seal, pictured at right, is an example of a clasping leaf.

Smooth Solomon's seal

Dyer's madder

Sometimes, three or more leaves grow from a common point of attachment. This style of leaf arrangement is called *whorled*, and is seen in the dyer's madder photo at left.

To the botanist, leaf attachment and leaf arrangement are different discussions; for the layperson, the distinction is not important. The whorled example seems to cross into both categories.

LEAF SHAPES

Leaves and leaflets take numerous shapes; here are the most common. Note that leaves may taper on one or both ends, may have rounded or heart-shaped bases with pointed tips, or any number of combinations.

Low bilberry

Oval leaves (sometimes called elliptic leaves) are the most familiar. At left are the oval leaves of low bilberries.

Lance-shaped or sword-like leaves are long and slender; often, sides are almost parallel for much of the leaves' length. Below left are the lance-shaped leaves of starry false Solomon's seal.

Paddle-shaped leaves are narrow at the base, widening at or above the midpoint; they typically have a rounded tip. Below right are the paddle-shaped leaves of barberry.

Starry false Solomon's seal

Barberry

SAFETY AND PLANT IDENTIFICATION

If you are using this book to identify plants just for pleasure, that's great; hopefully, you will find what you're looking for and may even enjoy keeping a life list of fruits spotted. However, if you are planning to eat any of the fruits you identify, it is critical to follow good identification practices. Before sampling a plant's fruit, determine the plant's overall structure, its color, its leaf and stem arrangement, fruit appearance and characteristics. The photos and text in this book are as clear and concise as possible; however, they are not exhaustive. Sometimes, a plant looks slightly different than those photographed, and identification becomes a bit of a guessing game. It's prudent to consult more than one guidebook before consuming something you've foraged, and I strongly urge you to do so. The Helpful Resources on pgs. 312–314 will give you some sources that may be helpful. This extra effort is worth it; a mistake could cause illness or, in rare cases, death.

It's also important to note that individual reaction to foods varies; to some, the everyday peanut is a ballpark snack, while to others, it can cause life-threatening complications if ingested. Reactions to wild foods are not always well-documented or predictable; when you're eating an unfamiliar wild food, try just a small portion at first.

Also, remember that many wild foods are edible only at a certain stage of growth, or with certain special preparations. That information is beyond the scope of this book; however, the notes and information with each species account point out possible issues with the various fruits you may find. If the text has any indications that special preparations may be required, or that ripeness is critical to edibility, it is your responsibility to learn what is required to make certain your foraged fruits are edible and safe.

Some fruits are edible but not palatable; these are noted as "edible" in most cases, although in a few cases they are noted as "not edible" because they really aren't worth experimenting with. Others may cause

stomach upset or other relatively minor difficulties; these are noted as "not edible." Some, however, can kill if enough is ingested; and in a few cases, the amount is shockingly little. These plants are listed as "toxic" and contain the skull-and-crossbones symbol at left. Pay attention to this. It's not worth taking chances.

WHAT IS NOT INCLUDED IN THIS BOOK

In general, the fruits included in this book are those which most people would identify as fruits. Capsules such as those produced by poppies, maple-tree wings (samaras), and dry seeds such as sunflower seeds and wheat kernels, would not likely be considered a fruit, so are not in this book. Here are some other things which are not included.

Nuts, such as these shagbark hickories, are large, dry fruits with hard seedcoats; they usually contain a single seed. Nuts are indehiscent, meaning that they remain closed when mature.

Legumes are pods, often quite narrow, that contain pea-like or bean-like seeds. Legumes are dehiscent, meaning that they dry out and split open, releasing their seeds. Pods of American vetch are pictured at left.

Follicles are dry, dehiscent fruits that dry out and split on one side to scatter their seeds. The fruit of a milkweed, a very common follicle, is pictured at left.

Galls are not a fruit, but rather a swelling in the stem of a plant caused by an insect. The round bulge on this anemone could be easily mistaken for a fruit.

BE CERTAIN, BE SAFE: WILD GRAPES

Wild grapes are a prime wild edible; they're delicious and abundant. However, several other vining plants in our area have inedible or toxic fruits that appear somewhat similar to wild grapes. Fortunately, it's easy to distinguish between them if you pay attention when harvesting.

Below is a photo of riverbank grapes (pg. 208). On the next page, you'll find photos of some fruits that appear similar. Key identification points also help you distinguish between grapes and these other fruits. When harvesting wild grapes, always be certain you know which plant the fruit you're picking is growing on; woodbine, for example, often intertwines with grape vines.

Riverbank grape

White bryony (pg. 206)

Silktassel (pg. 214)

Smilax (pg. 226)

Woodbine, Virginia creeper (pg. 228)

LEAVES

Grape: Three to five shallow to deep lobes, toothed edges

White bryony: Five to seven deep, curved lobes; several large teeth

Silktassel: Leathery oval leaves; smooth edges

Smilax: Heart-shaped or oval; smooth edges

Woodbine, Virginia creeper: Palmately compound (typically 5-part); coarsely toothed edges

TENDRILS

Grape: Coiling tendrils

White bryony: Long, unbranched tendrils

Silktassel: No tendrils

Smilax: Long, thin tendrils

Woodbine, Virginia creeper: Branched tendrils; Virginia creeper's tendrils have adhesive disks at tips

FRUITS

Grape: Purplish with a bloom; large, tight cluster on sturdy stalk; up to six teardrop-shaped seeds (delicious)

White bryony: Shiny, dark purple; four to six (typically) in a flat-topped cluster (highly toxic)

Silktassel: Small, egg-shaped, purplish with a bloom; long, hanging cluster (inedible)

Smilax: Bluish-black with a bloom; rounded cluster on stiff stalk (inedible)

Woodbine, Virginia creeper: Bluish-purple with a bloom; loose clusters on hot-pink stemlets (inedible)

HABITAT ZONES IN THE ROCKY MOUNTAIN STATES

The six states through which the Rocky Mountains extend have a wide variety of habitats, ranging from hot, dry deserts that are warm even in winter to mountain peaks that lie under a blanket of snow throughout the year. Idaho has the lowest elevation of the Rocky Mountain states—710 feet above sea level in Nez Perce county. Colorado's Mount Elbert, at 14,440 feet, is the highest point in our six-state area. In addition to tremendous differences in elevation, the area also covers a wide latitude; the Rocky Mountain states extend from the Canadian border down to the Mexican border. Average summertime high temperatures range from the 60s in parts of Montana to the 90s in parts of New Mexico.

The discussions of the species in this book all include information about the *habitat zone* each plant inhabits. In many cases, the habitat zone is defined primarily by elevation, but other factors also affect the habitat and the plant communities found there—even in the same state. For example, if you took an August hike at 9,500 feet in Rocky Mountain National Park in eastern Colorado, you would be well advised to carry a long-sleeved shirt and rain gear—higher elevations on the Front Range can be cool even at the height of summer, and afternoon rainstorms are an almost daily occurrence. Travel southwest about 150 miles (as the eagle flies) to Grand Mesa National Forest in western Colorado, however, and you'll probably want to wear shorts and a big-brimmed, sun-blocking hat when hiking at the same elevation to stay cool in the hot, dry environment of the Western Slope.

Brief descriptions of the habitat zones in the region are given on the next few pages. By observing the specific plants in the area you're hiking, you will soon learn to judge the zone you're in.

THE PLAINS

This term is used in this book to describe areas that are generally below 5,000 feet. Much of the eastern portions of Montana, Wyoming, Colorado and New Mexico are *grasslands*, semi-arid areas dominated by perennial grasses and scattered low shrubs; trees and larger shrubs grow in *riparian* areas along creeks, lakes and rivers. Annual precipitation is low in grasslands; summers are hot and dry, while winters are cold and windy with infrequent snow. Much of this land is used for agricultural purposes such as grazing and farming; croplands are generally irrigated.

Eastern foothills

THE FOOTHILLS

This is the transition zone between the plains and the true mountains; generally, the foothills range from 5,000 to 8,000 feet. Pinyon pine, juniper and ponderosa pine are the dominant conifers; Gambel oak and mountain mahogany are common deciduous species. Grasses and wildflowers cover much of the non-forested area, especially in the rolling foothills of the eastern part of our area.

In western Colorado and eastern Utah, the foothills transition zone is more likely to be *semi-desert shrubland*. This habitat, also called

Semi-desert shrublands

the high-desert plateau, is characterized by scrubby, drought-tolerant shrubs such as sagebrush, greasewood and saltbrush. Cacti such as prickly pear (pg. 116), yucca (pgs. 38, 40) and desert wildflowers are common; stunted junipers and pinyon pines, along with some fruit-bearing shrubs like serviceberry (pg. 216) and Fremont's mahonia (pg. 170), dot the landscape. The soil is sandy or rocky, and high winds frequently buffet the area.

Montane habitat

THE MONTANE ZONE
In this zone, which is typically from 8,000 to 9,500 feet, the vegetation gradually changes from scrub to tall forests. Conifers are larger than in the lower zones; they include Douglas fir, lodgepole pine and, in some montane areas, ponderosa pine. Quaking aspen trees replace Gambel oak as the dominant deciduous species. Wax currant (pg. 166) and buffaloberry (pg. 182) are common fruit-bearing shrubs; creeping grape-holly (pg. 224) is often found beneath taller trees. Average temperatures are lower in the montane zone than in the foothills; the area also receives much more snow.

Sub-alpine habitat

THE SUB-ALPINE ZONE

This zone is found from about 9,500 feet to the *treeline*, the altitude above which large trees no longer grow. The sub-alpine climate is more extreme than lower elevations, so the growing season is shorter and plants must adapt to harsh conditions, especially in winter. This is an area of conifers rather than deciduous trees. Engelmann spruce, sub-alpine fir, bristlecone pine and sometimes lodgepole pine grow in dense stands in this zone; in the warmer western and southern parts of our area, limber pine is also common. Acid-loving plants such as grouse whortleberry (pg. 144) and bilberries (pg. 230) grow under the tall pines.

Krummholz in the alpine zone

THE ALPINE ZONE

This is the zone above the treeline. Also called the *tundra*, this area is dominated by rocks, hardy wildflowers, grasses, lichens and scattered low shrubs. *Krummholz*, shrubs and trees that have been twisted by the fierce winds into shortened, gnarled shapes, are visible in this treeless region, and are often associated with the alpine zone. The elevation at which the treeline starts is influenced by summer temperatures; in areas that have warmer summers, the treeline is higher because the trees have a better chance of robust growth. In the Rockies, treeline ranges from less than 10,000 feet in Wyoming's Grand Teton National Park to over 11,500 feet in Colorado's Rocky Mountain National Park.

HOW TO USE THIS BOOK

1. When you find a plant with fruits, pay attention to **fruit color** first. Use the colored quarter-circles at the top corner of the left-hand pages to find the corresponding section.

SMALL
WOODY SHRUB

2. Next, identify the **form of the plant**: is it a tender leafy plant, a shrub (small or large?), a vine or a tree? Flip through the color section until you find the proper form, using the icon at the top of the page.

3. Look through the **photos** in this section and see if you find similar fruits. If you can't, look in the color sections before and after the section you're in; if you are looking at a red fruit, but don't see anything like it, go to the orange section or to the purple section. Color judgment is subjective, and individual specimens may vary slightly, so you may have to look for the fruit in several color sections.

Mountain ash

It's also possible that you've found unripe fruit, and since this book shows fruits in the ripe stage, you might not be looking in the right color section. Most fruits are green when immature, ripening to a

Whitebark raspberry

different color; but some pass through several colors before fully ripening. Whitebark raspberries (pg. 254), for example, start out green and ripen to black; in between they turn yellow, salmon-orange, bright red, and purplish-red. Other fruits undergo similar transformations. Once you find something that looks similar—even if it's the wrong color—proceed to the next step.

4. Look at the **range map** icon at the top of the page to determine whether the plant is found in your area. Use these range maps as an approximation, as there are few official sources of information pertaining to wild plants, and no resource is all-inclusive.

ALTERNATE LEAVES

5. When you find a photograph that appears similar to the fruit you've found (even if the color is not quite right), and the plant is the correct form, take a look at the **leaves** to see if they grow opposite one another on the stem, alternately on the stem, or in a whorl. This distinction is often the main key to properly identifying a plant.

6. Now read the full description, paying particular attention to any text that is in green; this color is used to point out key features that distinguish a plant from those with similar appearances. Also **study the "Compare"** section; here, you'll find information about plants that have similarities to the one pictured, along with page references for those which appear in this book. By following these references, you may sometimes find a photo showing the fruit you've found in a more ripened state; the description on that page will help you to identify the plant, even if you're looking at it in its unripe state.

SUMMER

7. To help determine when a fruit ripens, we've included a **season** icon at the top of the page. This will tell you the approximate season you're likely to find ripe berries or fruits and can help narrow down the possibilities when there are a number of look-alike fruits and berries.

8. Finally, the **thumb tab** at the top indicates whether a plant is toxic, not edible, edible, or delicious.

A species indicated as **toxic** has fruits that are highly poisonous and should not be eaten under any circumstances. The corresponding photo bears a skull-and-crossbones symbol for good reason; do not sample any part of a plant bearing this symbol. Species indicated as **not edible** bear fruit which, while not highly toxic, may cause sickness upon ingestion or have other negative side effects. Species indicated as **edible** bear fruits that are just that: edible. Some are bland but handy to know about as survival food, while others have a minor place in the forager's kitchen. Species indicated as **delicious** are the berries and fruits many people seek out. Raspberries, plums and choke-cherries are just a few of the many delicious wild fruits found in the Rocky Mountain states. Unlike the fruits simply marked as edible, these are the best wild edibles the region has to offer.

Here's an example; follow along to see if you can identify this fruit.

The plant has fruit that is primarily black, and it is a large shrub (you can't see that in the photo at left, but in the field, the form is obvious). Go to the black section of the book (starting on pg. 246), and flip to the beginning of the section that lists large shrubs (pg. 260).

LARGE
WOODY SHRUB

Twenty-one large shrubs (or large shrubs/small trees) are listed in the black section. Himalayan blackberry can be eliminated, because the fruit doesn't look at all like those on your plant.

ALTERNATE
LEAVES

You notice that the leaves on your plant are alternate, spaced along the stem rather than across from one another. This eliminates twinberry honeysuckle, European privet, common buckthorn and nannyberry. Sixteen species remain as possibilities.

The leaves on your plant are oval to egg-shaped; this eliminates the currants (golden, sticky and prickly currants) and the gooseberries (trumpet, Canadian and whitestem) because their leaves are lobed. Allthorn and

Warnock's snakewood have oval leaves, but they are very tiny so they do not match your plant.

Eight choices remain: black chokecherry (pg. 270); western sand cherry (pg. 272); Rocky Mountain elderberry (pg. 274); mountain huckleberry (pg. 276); Smith's buckthorn (pg. 282); cotoneaster (pg. 290) and Cascara and glossy buckthorn (pg. 294). The fruit of western sand cherry are much larger than yours, so that is eliminated.

The leaves on the remaining plants are all somewhat similar: oval or oblong with toothy edges. Looking at the fruits, however, you notice that those on your plant are growing in a large, hanging cluster. Most of the plants remaining on your list have fruits that grow singly or in small clusters, so they are no longer possibilities. That leaves two choices: black chokecherry and Rocky Mountain elderberry.

Looking more closely at the photo and description for Rocky Mountain elderberry, you realize that it has compound leaves, but your plant has simple leaves. Studying the text on the chokecherry page, it seems likely that you've found a chokecherry.

To confirm your identification, study the "Compare" text on pg. 270 to see what other plants resemble this one. Looking at the photo of pin cherry (pg. 188), you see that although the fruits are similar and grow in a cluster, they are bright red; your plant has a few reddish fruits but it is clear that the fruits on your plant will be much darker when ripe; in addition, the leaves on the pin cherry are much narrower. The leaves do look like those of the serviceberry (pg. 216), but the fruit is not similar.

You've found black chokecherry, a delicious wild edible fruit.

Once you've identified your wild fruit or berry, check the bottom of the page, as we've included a reference to our companion book, *Cooking with Wild Berries & Fruits of the Rocky Mountain States,* which includes delicious recipes, handy tips, and many different ways to put your newly found edible fruits and berries to use.

SMALL
WOODY SHRUB

ALTERNATE
LEAVES

LATE SUMMER
TO EARLY FALL

Common Name

Scientific name

HABITAT: General environment in which the plant is typically found in our area, including light and moisture requirements

GROWTH: The growth form of the plant in our area, ranging from small, tender plants, to vines, to small or large shrubs, to trees

LEAVES: Description of the plant's leaves, including leaf style and shape, arrangement on the plant, attachment to the main stem, and color of the leaves

FRUIT: Description of the fruit, including type (berry, pome, drupe or other), color, arrangement, appearance and edibility information

SEASON: When the plant bears ripe fruit in our area

COMPARE: Plants or fruits with similar attributes, including characteristics that differentiate them

NOTES: Interesting facts about the plant, including harvesting tips for edible plants, notes on other parts of the plant that may be edible, historical or modern-day medicinal uses, and miscellaneous tips and facts

TENDER
LEAFY PLANT

ALTERNATE
LEAVES

MIDSUMMER
THROUGH
EARLY FALL

Cutleaf Nightshade

Solanum triflorum

HABITAT: This native annual inhabits sunny, weedy areas, including prairies, dry shrublands, waste ground, agricultural areas, prairie dog colonies and roadsides; also found on disturbed sites and occasionally in juniper forests. It grows from the plains through the montane zones.

GROWTH: A coarse-textured, low-spreading plant that branches numerous times. Individual stems may be up to 24 inches long, but they typically trail along the ground; the plant is rarely more than a foot high. All parts of the plant have a foul scent.

LEAVES: The long, thick, sparsely hairy leaves are divided into multiple lobes with deep sinuses (the rounded depression between the lobes); they resemble thick dandelion leaves with rounded teeth. Leaves are up to 2 inches long and about two-thirds as wide; they grow alternately on thick, hairy petioles (stemlets).

FRUIT: Round, smooth berries about ½ inch across, with star-shaped caps that curl away from the fruit, grow in clusters of up to three fruits on stalks that originate in leaf axils. Both young and mature fruits are green with pale stripes; ripe fruits are lighter green than underripe fruits. As with eastern black nightshade (pg. 250), there is debate about their edibility. According to the *Thirtieth Annual Report of the Bureau of American Ethnology to the Secretary of the Smithsonian Institution* (Smithsonian Institution, 1908–1909), Zuñi Indians made a chili-spiked "condiment" from ripe fruits, and some modern sources list the fruits as edible (most seem to be based on the Smithsonian report). Other sources list them as toxic, especially when unripe. Since ripeness is hard to judge in a berry that remains green, it is wise to consider the fruit inedible.

SEASON: White flowers are present from early to late summer; berries are on the plant from midsummer through early fall.

COMPARE: Buffalobur nightshade (*S. rostratum*) has similar leaves, but its fruits are covered with long spines; its range is similar to cutleaf's.

NOTES: Cutleaf nightshade is considered a noxious agricultural pest.

green = key identification feature

TENDER
LEAFY PLANT

ALTERNATE
LEAVES

SUMMER
THROUGH FALL

Sacred
jimsonweed

Thorn
apple

Jimsonweed (several)

Datura spp.

HABITAT: Two jimsonweed appear in our region: *Datura wrightii*, sacred jimsonweed (pictured at right), and *D. stramonium*, the common variety, which is also called thorn apple. Both are found in sunny pastures, waste ground, agricultural areas and road ditches; they grow from the plains through the lower foothills, and are common in semi-desert shrublands.

GROWTH: An erect annual plant, generally 2 to 4 feet tall and bushy, with smooth, **purplish stems that fork repeatedly**. Each fork bears a white or pale lavender flower shaped like a deep, angular funnel with well-defined edges and sharp tips. The flowers have a pleasant scent, but all other parts of the plant have a foul odor, especially when crushed.

LEAVES: Alternate, dark green on top, lighter underneath, generally 4 to 6 inches long. Sacred jimsonweed leaves typically have **wavy edges and shallow or non-existent lobes**. Thorn-apple leaves have **pointed, irregular teeth and several lobes**; they resemble an elongated maple or red-oak leaf.

FRUIT: Sacred jimsonweed fruit is globe-like, up to 1½ inches; it grows from the stem fork on a **drooping stemlet**. Thorn-apple fruit is more egg-shaped, about 2 inches long, growing **upright** from the fork. Fruits of both are **covered in spiny prickles**; they are green when young, turning brown and splitting to scatter seeds. All parts of both plants are toxic.

SEASON: Jimsonweed flowers throughout summer and into fall; fruits develop from the flower remnants throughout the season.

COMPARE: Pricklypoppy (*Argemone* spp.), which in found in similar habitats in our area, has an egg-shaped spiny fruit growing upright on the stem, but its leaves are prickly with multiple lobes; it is much less bushy.

NOTES: Thorn apple is non-native; it was noted in Jamestown, Virginia, during colonial days. Although sacred jimsonweed is a native plant, both it and thorn apple are considered pests in agricultural areas; cattle can be poisoned if they graze on the plants. Both contain scopolamine, atropine and hyoscyamine, powerful alkaloids that cause hallucinations, various physical difficulties, and, occasionally, death.

green = key identification feature

TENDER
VINE

ALTERNATE
LEAVES

LATE SUMMER
THROUGH FALL

Wild Cucumber
–OR– Balsam Apple

Echinocystis lobata

HABITAT: This native plant prefers sunny, moist locations, including stream-banks, moist thickets and woods, roadsides, swamp edges. Wild cucumber is found on the plains.

GROWTH: Wild cucumber is a non-woody vining plant with coiled tendrils; leaf nodes are sometimes hairy. The vine grows rapidly, and can reach 25 feet in length.

LEAVES: Alternating leaves, somewhat resembling maple leaves, grow on long petioles (stemlets); each typically has five distinct triangular lobes, but may have as few as three or as many as seven lobes. Leaves are smooth and bright green; edges may have very fine hairs (visible with a lens).

FRUIT: A pulpy green berry-like fruit with a firm skin (called a *pepo*), 1 to 2 inches long, roughly egg-shaped, sometimes with blunt ends, grows on a short stalk from the leaf node. The fruit has supple, spiny prickles overall. Eventually the fruit dries out and turns brown, splitting open at the end to disperse its four seeds. The fruit is inedible.

SEASON: Wild cucumber blooms in mid to late summer, producing a profusion of lacy white flowers that may blanket the surrounding vegetation; fruits are present from late summer through fall.

COMPARE: Riverbank grapes (pg. 208) are woody vining plants with similar leaves, but their fruits are purple and grow in clusters like the familiar commercial grape.

NOTES: The roots of wild cucumber have been used medicinally to treat ailments including headache, stomach problems, rheumatism and even love-sickness. According to *Native American Ethnobotany* (Daniel E. Moerman; Timber Press), the seeds were used as beads by American Indian peoples.

green = key identification feature

SMALL WOODY
SUBSHRUB

BASAL
LEAVES

SUMMER

Soapweed

Spanish
bayonet

Narrowleaf
yucca

Dry-Fruited Yucca (several)

Yucca spp.

HABITAT: Several native yuccas with non-fleshy fruits that dry out and split open grow in our area. All inhabit hot, dry areas such as grasslands, mesa tops, exposed slopes and open woodlands. They grow from the plains through the foothills and are common in semi-desert shrublands.

GROWTH: Yuccas are subshrubs; the three discussed here have inconspicuous woody stems and their clusters of evergreen leaves appear to grow directly from the ground. A flowering stalk rises from the cluster, and numerous cream-colored flowers are attached to the stalk on short stemlets; some, particularly those of Spanish bayonet, have a purple tinge. Stalks of soapweed (*Yucca glauca*) and Spanish bayonet (*Y. harrimaniae*) are generally 2 to 2½ feet tall; Spanish bayonet's may grow to 4½ feet. Flowering stalks of narrowleaf yucca (*Y. angustissima*) are generally 3 to 4 feet tall, but may grow to 6 feet. Yuccas often grow in colonies.

LEAVES: Stiff, sword-shaped leaves grow in a basal fashion; they are dull green with white or brownish edges. Tips come to a sharp point; edges have thread-like filaments that are curly or wavy. Leaves of Spanish bayonet and narrowleaf yucca are up to 20 inches long; soapweed's may be up to 3½ feet. Leaves of narrowleaf and soapleaf yucca are generally no more than ½ inch wide; Spanish bayonet's may be up to 1½ inches wide.

FRUIT: Lumpy, rounded capsules are attached to the stalk on short stemlets. Fruits are generally 1¼ to 2¼ inches long and are green when young, turning brown and splitting apart when mature. They are not edible.

SEASON: Fruits are green most of the summer, drying out and splitting open in late summer; dry, split capsules persist through the next season.

COMPARE: Banana yucca (pg. 40) is similar, but its fruits are fleshy and grow on branches that radiate from the main stalk. Parry's agave (*Agave parryi*) has similar, inedible fruits, but its leaves are much shorter and wider; in our area, it is found only in southern New Mexico.

NOTES: Yucca can be used as a soap substitute; fibers from the leaves are used to make rope. Soapweed is the state flower of New Mexico.

green = key identification feature

Dried and green fruits

Narrowleaf yucca

SMALL WOODY
SUBSHRUB

BASAL
LEAVES

MID TO
LATE SUMMER

Banana Yucca

Yucca baccata

HABITAT: This native perennial is found in hot, dry areas such as grasslands, mesa tops, exposed slopes and open conifer forests. It grows from the plains through the foothills, and is common in semi-desert shrublands.

GROWTH: A subshrub, with an inconspicuous woody stem at its center. Its cluster of evergreen leaves appears to grow directly from the ground; a flowering stalk rises from the cluster, producing numerous cream-colored or red-tinged flowers that grow in a loose, branched cluster. The flowering stalk is often the same height as the surrounding leaves, although it may be up to 3 feet tall. Yucca often grows in colonies.

LEAVES: Stiff, sword-shaped leaves, 12 to 24 inches long, grow in a basal fashion; they are bluish-green with white or brownish edges. Leaves are concave, 1 to 2 inches across. The tips come to a sharp point; edges have numerous thread-like filaments that are curly or wavy.

FRUIT: Technically a capsule, the fruit is very fleshy and almost squash-like in appearance; it has smooth green skin most of the season and is typically 3 to 6 inches long but sometimes longer. Mature fruits have a reddish tinge; they have tight columns of flat black seeds inside (some seeds are white), surrounded by whitish flesh. Unlike the non-fleshy yuccas (pg. 38), banana yucca fruits do not dry out and split open when mature. Ripe fruits can be eaten raw or cooked. Pueblo Indians prepared them in a variety of ways, often preserving cooked, mashed fruit for later use.

SEASON: Fruits ripen in mid to late summer; early Indians often picked the fruits when still green to beat wild animals to the harvest.

COMPARE: Torrey's yucca (*Y. torreyi*) has similar fleshy, edible fruits, but its fruits are smaller than banana yucca's; in our area, it is found only in southern New Mexico. Other yuccas (pg. 38) also grow in our area but the fruits are not fleshy and the flowering stalk is generally much taller; fruits from these yuccas are not considered edible.

NOTES: For a good description of yucca and its many uses, see *Edible Native Plants of the Rocky Mountains* by H. D. Harrington.

green = key identification feature

CACTUS

MID TO
LATE SUMMER

Spinystar

Escobaria vivipara

HABITAT: This native cactus inhabits sunny, well-drained areas such as plains, grasslands, rocky ridges and hillsides; it also grows in cracks between boulders, and under sparse shrubs or conifers. It is found from the plains through the montane zones, and is common in semi-desert shrublands.

GROWTH: Spinystar are *stem succulents*, non-woody plants that hold water in their soft tissue. They are typically less than 3 inches tall and nearly spherical when young; older plants are more cylindrical and may be up to 6 inches tall. The surface is covered with rounded, pillowy bumps called *tubercles*; each is crowned with an *areole*, a rounded, tuft-like bud. Each areole has 3 to 14 straight, brownish spines up to 1 inch long that grow in an upright spray from the center; these upright spines are surrounded by a ring of up to 40 shorter spines that lie flat. Spinystar produce several many-petaled flowers up to 1 inch across that grow from the top of the plant; flowers are typically pink with yellow centers.

LEAVES: No normal leaves; the spines may be considered modified leaves.

FRUIT: The oblong, rounded, pale green pod-like berries are up to 1 inch long and one-third as wide; they grow upright from the top of the plants, poking out between the spines. The fruits have smooth skins and a brown floral remnant at the end. They may develop reddish-purple blotches when fully mature, or may remain completely green. The interior of the fruit is green and soft; a cavity in the center is filled with brown seeds and juicy, gel-like pulp. The fruits are edible and reported to be delicious.

SEASON: Spinystar flowers from early through late summer; fruits follow, ripening from mid to late summer.

COMPARE: Missouri foxtail cactus (*E. missouriensis*) is similar in overall appearance, but its flowers are greenish-yellow and its ripe fruits are solid red on the outside with black seeds; in this area, it is found scattered throughout various counties, but is most common south of the Bitterroot Mountains in Idaho and Montana, and in northwestern New Mexico.

NOTES: Some sources refer to this cactus as *Coryphantha vivipara*.

green = key identification feature

SMALL
WOODY SHRUB

ALTERNATE
LEAVES

EARLY TO
MID SUMMER

*see below

Gooseberries (green stage) (several)

Ribes spp.

HABITAT: Three native gooseberry species are fairly common in much of our area: trumpet (*Ribes leptanthum*), Canadian (*R. oxyacanthoides*) and whitestem (*R. inerme*). Gooseberries inhabit thickets and tangled areas, scrubby shelterbelts, rocky areas, and rich, moist woods, especially those along rivers or ponds; depending on variety, they grow from the plains through the sub-alpine zones.

GROWTH: An arching shrub, 3 to 5 feet high. Canadian gooseberry stems have numerous prickles between the leaf nodes; mature stems of trumpet and whitestem gooseberries are usually smooth between nodes but may have scattered bristles. Leaf nodes have one to three sharp thorns.

LEAVES: Attached alternately to the stem by a petiole (stemlet). Each leaf has three to five distinct lobes, resembling a rounded maple leaf. Trumpet gooseberry leaves are ¾ inch long or shorter; Canadian and whitestem gooseberry leaves are about 1½ inches long.

FRUIT: The ¼- to ½-inch round berry grows singly or in clusters of two or three. Fruits of all three are smooth-skinned and have distinct stripes that run longitudinally; a prominent flower remnant, often called a pigtail, is present at the end of the berry. Gooseberries are green when young; the species listed here are black when ripe.

SEASON: Fruit is green but edible from early summer through midsummer.

COMPARE: Currant shrubs (pgs. 142, 166, 232, 256, 262, 278, 280) resemble gooseberry shrubs, but fruits are borne in racemes (long clusters of multiple fruits).

NOTES: Green gooseberries are rich in pectin, and are used primarily for jam, jelly and pie. Taste a few before harvesting; they will be sour, but if they are too astringent, let them mature a bit longer before picking. When the fruits ripen (pgs. 172, 264, 266, 268), they are excellent in baked desserts, sauces and other dishes.

green = key identification feature

*combined range

Whitestem gooseberry

LARGE
WOODY SHRUB

OPPOSITE
LEAVES

MID TO
LATE SUMMER

Cliff Fendlerbush

Fendlera rupicola

HABITAT: This native plant inhabits rocky areas, and is often found growing in crevices on steep slopes and canyon ledges; it also grows on mesas and rocky hillsides, and in scrubby desert areas. It tolerates drought and high temperatures, and inhabits the foothills through the montane zone.

GROWTH: An open shrub with an upright, narrow form, cliff fendlerbush is generally 3 to 6 feet tall, although it can be up to 9 feet tall. Young stems are tan or pale gray and typically ridged; older stems have shreddy, dark gray bark.

LEAVES: Thick, narrow leaves with a prominent midvein grow oppositely or in bunched clusters on very short petioles (stemlets). Leaves are up to 1½ inches long and about one-fifth as wide; edges are untoothed. Undersides are pale green; fine hairs may be present on both sides.

FRUIT: The four-chambered capsule looks like an elongated green acorn with four petals flaring out around its base. The capsule is about ½ inch long and half as wide at its base, tapering to a short point. It develops a red blush as it matures; when fully mature, it turns brown and splits into four parts to release its seeds. The fruits are regarded as inedible.

SEASON: In spring through early summer, cliff fendlerbush produces masses of white flowers, whose fallen, paddle-shaped petals blanket the surrounding ground. Fruits mature in mid to late summer.

COMPARE: Wright's fendlerbush (*F. wrightii*, which some sources consider to be the same as *F. rupicola*) has smaller leaves that are whitish underneath, and mature fruits that are reddish; in our area, it is found in southwestern Colorado and northwestern New Mexico. Cliff fendlerbush is sometimes called false mockorange because its appearance is similar to mockorange (*Philadelphus* spp.). Mockorange is generally a shorter plant with wider leaves and reddish-brown or tan bark; its fruits are smaller and more flattened than those of cliff fendlerbush.

NOTES: *Rupicola* means "rock dweller," a reference to this plant's rock-loving habits.

green = key identification feature

Cliff fendlerbush

Wright's fendlerbush

TREE

ALTERNATE
LEAVES

MID TO
LATE SUMMER

Common Pear

Pyrus communis

HABITAT: This is the common orchard pear, which has escaped cultivation and is found in scattered spots in the wild. Pears may be "planted" by anglers, hunters or picnickers who throw out a core after eating a commercial pear, so they are found near boat launches, parks and hiking trails. Pears do best in sunny areas with rich, moist, well-drained soil. They are most likely to be found from the plains through the foothills.

GROWTH: A medium to large tree, with a straight trunk and an open, spreading crown. Unlike orchard pears, which are grafted onto shorter stock to make picking easy, wild pears grow from seed, and tend to be taller than their domestic cousins. The trunk has furrowed grayish bark. Branches are reddish-brown to grayish; most are smooth, with visible gray lenticels (breathing pores), but side branches often have wrinkled bark or are knobby-looking. Pear trees have no thorns.

LEAVES: Glossy, thick, leathery leaves, up to 4 inches long and two-thirds as wide, grow alternately or in clusters on long yellowish-green petioles (stemlets). Leaves have pointed tips and are broadest near the base or below the midpoint; they often fold in slightly along the midline. Edges are finely serrated, and may appear wavy.

FRUIT: A greenish to yellowish pome, generally 1 to 2 inches across; the skin is rough, with fine brown patches or tiny dots. Pears grow on a thick stemlet and have a crown on the bottom. Unlike commercial pears, wild pears have little or no neck; they often grow with the crown end up, looking like a large, rough-skinned crabapple. Wild pears are generally firmer than domestic pears, but taste similar. There are no toxic look-alikes that have a crown on the bottom.

SEASON: Wild pears ripen in mid to late summer.

COMPARE: Feral apples (pg. 202) have similar leaves, but the fruits look like commercial apples.

NOTES: Wild pears may fall off the tree before fully ripe, but will ripen if left on the countertop for a few days.

green = key identification feature

TREE

ALTERNATE
LEAVES

LATE SUMMER
TO EARLY FALL

Osage Orange
–OR– Hedge Apple

Maclura pomifera

HABITAT: Open sunny areas and rich bottomlands are prime habitat; also found in pastures, and along fencerows and riverbanks. Osage orange is a plains and grassland species, and not found at higher elevations.

GROWTH: A deciduous tree up to 40 feet high with approximately equal width. Osage orange has many branches, and the foliage is dense, giving the appearance of a very solid tree. The trunk has brown bark with strong vertical fissures and orange patches. Only female trees bear fruit, and not until they are about 10 years old.

LEAVES: Bright green oblong leaves, 3 to 7 inches long, grow alternately on the stems. Leaves are smooth and glossy, with a rounded base and sharply pointed tip; although the edges are smooth, the leaves tend to curl upwards along the edges and may appear wavy. Half-inch-long thorns grow at leaf nodules. If a leaf or thorn is pulled off, milky sap will appear on the stem (careful; the sap may irritate the skin).

FRUIT: The pebbly-textured, leathery sphere, 4 to 6 inches across, consists of a pithy core surrounded by abundant small seeds. The fruit is light green with fine hairs when immature, ripening to hairless yellowish-green with a mild orange scent. Osage orange fruit is generally regarded as mildly toxic; sap from the fruit can cause skin irritation.

SEASON: Osage orange blooms in early summer; the large, round fruit grows throughout summer, ripening in late summer to early fall.

COMPARE: Nothing in our area resembles the fruit of the Osage orange.

NOTES: Osage orange is named after the Osage, an American Indian tribe that inhabited the tree's native range in Oklahoma and portions of the surrounding states. It is not native to our area, having been introduced as a hedge plant. Some people place the fruits around the house foundation or near windows to repel insects. The fruit also provides food for squirrels that shred it and strip the slimy husk off the seeds before eating them.

green = key identification feature

Mature fruit
and thorns

TENDER
LEAFY PLANT

ALTERNATE
COMPOUND
LEAVES

MID TO
LATE SUMMER

Austrian Peaweed

Sphaerophysa salsula

HABITAT: This introduced plant grows as a weed in disturbed areas, along roadsides, in fencerows and irrigation ditches, on mountain slopes and on waste ground. It is also a common pest in croplands, where it has become established when its seeds were accidentally mixed in with alfalfa seeds, which have a similar appearance. It grows from the plains through the montane zone.

GROWTH: A perennial, upright branching plant, generally up to 2 feet tall but occasionally taller; Austrian peaweed spreads by rhizomes (underground root-bearing stems) as well as by seed. It has a woody taproot that can reach down for water, allowing it to grow in dry areas. Red, pea-like flowers appear from late spring through midsummer, growing in leaf axils near the end of the stem.

LEAVES: Pinnately compound leaves grow alternately. Each leaf has a grooved stem that is up to 3¼ inches long, and 15 to 23 oval leaflets that are up to ¾ inch long. Upper surfaces of the leaflets are smooth; the undersides are covered with short white hairs.

FRUIT: Oval, bladder-like fruits, ½ to 1⅓ inches long and about half as wide, grow from the leaf axils near the end of the stem. Ripe fruits range from pale to rich yellow, and may have a slight reddish blush. One edge of the fruit has a groove-like seam. The fruits are inedible.

SEASON: Fruits are ripe from mid to late summer.

COMPARE: Ground-plum milkvetch (pg. 82) has similar but much smaller leaves that grow at the ends of the stems; its fruit is more solid and is reddish when ripe. Bladderpod (pg. 88) has inflated, bladder-like fruits, but it is a low, ground-hugging plant.

NOTES: This Asian native is a vigorous grower whose range is increasing. It is generally considered a noxious, invasive weed. It is also referred to as alkali swainsonpea or red bladder-vetch; the latter name is a reference to the color of its flowers.

green = key identification feature

TENDER
LEAFY PLANT

ALTERNATE
LEAVES

MID TO
LATE SUMMER

*see below

Ground Cherries (several)

Physalis spp.

HABITAT: Fields, slopes, rocky areas, mesas and waste ground; often found along fences, streams and railroad grades. They grow from the plains through the foothills, and are found in semi-desert shrublands.

GROWTH: A very leafy plant, 1 to 4 feet in height. A dozen varieties grow in our area. Depending on variety, ground cherry grows as a perennial from a rhizome (underground root-bearing stem), or as an annual from a taproot. In our area, common perennials include the clammy (*Physalis heterophylla*), ivyleaf (*P. hederifolia*), longleaf (*P. longifolia*), prairie (*P. hispida*) and Virginia (*P. virginiana*) ground cherry; downy ground cherry (*P. pubescens*) is an annual. All ground cherries listed here are native plants.

LEAVES: Alternate, on short to medium petioles (stemlets). Leaf shapes are highly variable; leaves of some species have large, irregular teeth, but others are smooth-edged or slightly wavy.

FRUIT: A round, many-seeded berry, ½ to ¾ inch across, is enclosed in a ribbed husk that hangs from a leaf axil or stem fork; husks of most species have 10 equally spaced ribs that may be subtle. Berries of the listed species are yellow to orangish, and edible, when fully ripe. *Unripe berries and all other parts of the plant, including the papery husk, are toxic.*

SEASON: Yellow bell-shaped flowers, generally with dark spots inside the base, are present all summer; the berries ripen in mid to late summer.

COMPARE: Purple ground cherry (pg. 56) is similar, but its flowers are purple.

NOTES: Key features help identify individual species. Clammy ground cherry plants have sticky hairs overall; leaves are wide with rounded teeth or wavy edges. Ivyleaf ground cherry leaves are narrow with large, rounded teeth or wavy edges. Longleaf, prairie and Virginia ground cherry have narrow leaves that often lack teeth. Longleaf ground cherry leaves often have an asymmetrical base and the stem is grooved. Prairie ground cherry leaves are finely hairy on both surfaces, while longleaf and Virginia ground cherry leaves are generally smooth. Downy ground cherry have heart-shaped leaves; husks have five sharply distinct ribs.

green = key identification feature   *combined range

Ripe ground cherries

Clammy ground cherry

Longleaf ground cherry

Husks shown contain unripe green berries (all parts of the plant are toxic at this stage)

TENDER
LEAFY PLANT

ALTERNATE
LEAVES

SUMMER
THROUGH FALL

Purple Ground Cherry

Quincula lobata

HABITAT: This native plant grows in dry, sunny areas that have sandy or gravelly soil, including prairies, woodland edges and openings, mesas, plains, washes, open hillsides, roadsides, waste areas and canyons. In our area, it is found in the plains, foothills and semi-desert shrubland zones.

GROWTH: Purple ground cherry spreads sideways rather than up; it is generally less than 6 inches tall, although individual stems may be 18 inches long. It grows from a rhizome (underground root-bearing stem) and often forms large, mat-like colonies. Stems and leaves are covered with small hairs, each tipped with a tiny, crystal-like bladder (visible with a lens). Purple ground cherry is tolerant of drought and simply goes dormant during dry spells, but when it rains, the plants resume blooming; this cycle continues from spring until the first frost. After a rain, flattened purple flowers, ½ to 1 inch across, blanket the plant; they resemble petunias.

LEAVES: Dark green leaves up to 3 inches long grow alternately or in small clusters, attached directly to the stem; the base of the leaf narrows to a stem-like neck. Edges are usually wavy and have large, rounded teeth. Leaves are covered with tiny, bladder-tipped hairs as described above.

FRUIT: A round berry, ½ to ¾ inch across, is enclosed in a papery, ribbed husk that hangs from a leaf axil; husks have five equally spaced ribs. The berry is yellow when ripe; it is edible and sweet when fully ripe, and is used to make jam or jelly. Foragers must always look for the purple flowers and bladder-tipped hairs to ensure accurate identification. *Unripe berries and all other parts of the plant, including the papery husk, are toxic.*

SEASON: Fruits are present throughout the growing season, ripening several weeks after the flowers open.

COMPARE: Other ground cherries (*Physalis* spp.; pg. 54) have similar ribbed, papery husks containing edible yellow berries, but none have large purple flowers, or bladder-tipped hairs on the leaves and stems.

NOTES: Purple ground cherry is sometimes called Chinese lantern; it was originally included in the *Physalis* family, as *P. lobata*.

green = key identification feature

Developing husk

Husks shown contain unripe green berries (all parts of the plant are toxic at this stage)

Husks with fruit

TENDER
LEAFY PLANT

ALTERNATE
LEAVES

MID TO
LATE SUMMER

Silverleaf Nightshade

Solanum elaeagnifolium

HABITAT: This native, weedy plant thrives in sunny, hot areas, including waste ground, agricultural fields, railroad grades, grasslands and over-grazed pastures. It can survive dry summers and grows in areas with little rainfall. In our area, it is found in the plains, foothills and semi-desert shrubland zones.

GROWTH: A multi-branched perennial, silverleaf nightshade can grow to 3 feet in height, although it is usually shorter. Stems are round and covered with flattened, downy hairs; a few scattered prickles are often present. Stems become woody at the base. Five-pointed purple flowers with yellow centers appear throughout the summer. The leaves die back in late summer or early fall, but the fruits typically persist through winter, appearing into the next growing season on leafless, woody stems.

LEAVES: Narrow, wavy-edged leaves grow alternately on thick, ½-inch peti-oles (stemlets). Leaves are generally 1 to 4 inches long and one-quarter as wide; they are dark green above and pale, dusty grayish-green underneath. Like the stems, the leaves and petioles are covered with downy hairs which give the plant an overall silvery appearance.

FRUIT: Round, juicy berries, up to ½ inch across with a cap shaped like a long-fingered crown, grow on long stemlets, singly or in small clusters; a single plant can produce as many as 60 fruits. Immature berries are green with dark blotches, ripening to yellow or orangish. The berries are toxic.

SEASON: Berries mature in mid to late summer, and persist through winter.

COMPARE: Two related plants with yellow fruits also grow in our area; they lack the silvery appearance. Carolina horsenettle (*S. carolinense*; in our area, found in scattered locations in Idaho, Utah, Colorado and New Mexico) has lobed leaves with thorns along the veins; its flowers are white. Melon leaf nightshade (*S. heterodoxum*; in our area, found primarily in scattered locations in New Mexico) has deeply lobed leaves with frilly edges; its stems are heavily covered with spines.

NOTES: Silverleaf nightshade is classed as a noxious weed in Idaho.

green = key identification feature

CACTUS

LATE SUMMER

Tree cholla

Rat-tail cholla

Tree Cholla –AND– Rat-Tail Cholla *Cylindropuntia* spp.

HABITAT: These two similar native cacti are found in dry, sunny areas with sandy or gravelly soil, such as hillsides, mesa tops, grasslands and desert flats. They grow from the plains through the foothills, and are common in semi-desert shrublands.

GROWTH: Both are much-branching plants with abundant spines. Tree cholla (*Cylindropuntia imbricata*) gets its common name from its potential height—up to 15 feet high in rare instances, although it is typically 4 to 6 feet tall; larger specimens have a tree-like trunk. Rat-tail cholla (*C. whipplei*; also called Whipple cholla) is a shorter plant, typically 2 feet tall or shorter; it often grows as a thicket. Cholla are composed of segments, often called joints, that branch off the main stem and each other. The segments are well armed with sharp spines that radiate from *areoles*, rounded tuft-like buds spaced evenly along the skin; tree cholla areoles typically have 8 to 15 spines each, while rat-tail cholla areoles typically have 3 to 8. Fine, barbed bristles called *glochids* also grow from the areoles. Tree cholla display numerous magenta-pink or purplish flowers at the ends of joints; rat-tail cholla have yellow flowers.

LEAVES: No normal leaves; spines may be considered modified leaves.

FRUIT: The cup-shaped, thick-skinned fruit has vertical or spiraling ridges, with very small, sharp spines and numerous bumps; the top has a bowl-like depression. Ripe fruits of both species are yellow with a greenish tinge; tree cholla's fruits are 1 to 1¾ inches long and wide, while rat-tail cholla's are ¾ to 1¼ inches long and two-thirds as wide. The fruits are sweet and edible when fully ripe; they are very seedy inside, and are usually stewed for use in jam-making.

SEASON: Flowers appear in late spring to early summer. Fruits develop in summer, ripening in late summer; they persist until the following season.

COMPARE: Christmas cactus (pg. 120) is related, but its ripe fruits are red.

NOTES: Harvest of cholla is restricted in some areas. Some texts list the cholla species as *Opuntia* rather than *Cylindropuntia*.

green = key identification feature

Tree cholla

CACTUS   FALL TO
                WINTER

Fishhook Barrel Cactus

Ferocactus wislizeni

HABITAT: This native cactus grows in hot, dry rocky or sandy areas. It is found in desert grasslands and shrubby desert areas, at elevations ranging from the plains through the low foothills. It cannot tolerate freezing.

GROWTH: A stout, ribbed, unbranched cactus that typically grows as a solo specimen rather than in a cluster. Younger barrel cacti are ball shaped and up to 1 foot across; older barrel cacti are columnar, typically 3 to 6 feet tall and up to 2 feet wide. The ribs have an abundance of spine clusters; each cluster has 3 or 4 thick, hooked spines up to 2 inches long, surrounded by up to 20 thinner, shorter spines. Older specimens tend to twist towards the south, giving barrel cactus one of its other common names, compass cactus.

LEAVES: No normal leaves; the spines may be considered modified leaves.

FRUIT: Each cactus has numerous fruits in a crown at the top. The egg-shaped fruit, up to 2 inches long, is green when immature, ripening to lemon-yellow. The fruit has numerous scales on the skin; an upright crown of dried floral remnants at the top makes it resemble a small lemon-yellow pineapple. Although edible, the fruit is somewhat dry, sour and seedy; the pulp can be roasted like squash or used to make jelly, candy or a lemonade-type beverage. There are no toxic look-alikes.

SEASON: In summer, bright orange or reddish flowers grow on top of the greenish fruits. As the fruits mature, the flowers dry up but remain attached to the fruit. Fruits ripen from fall to winter, often persisting on the plants through the following season.

COMPARE: California barrel cactus (*F. cylindraceus,* sometimes listed as *F. acanthodes*) is a close relative, but its large spines are curved rather than hooked; in our area it is found only in extreme southwestern Utah.

NOTES: The flesh of the main cactus body is simmered with sugar to make candy; in the past, barrel cacti were hollowed out to make containers. Barrel cacti grow very slowly and are considered threatened in the wild; transplanting wild specimens is restricted or forbidden in many places.

green = key identification feature

TENDER VINE   ALTERNATE LEAVES   FALL

Buffalo Gourd

Cucurbita foetidissima

HABITAT: This native perennial thrives in hot, dry areas with sandy soil, such as edges of agricultural fields, waste ground, grasslands, pastures and prairies. It grows from the plains through the lower montane zones.

GROWTH: A coarse, sprawling vine; stems may be up to 20 feet long, but the plant rarely rises more than a foot above the ground. Stems are thick, ridged and pale green; they extend outward from the center like the legs of a spider. All parts of the plant emit a foul, sweat-like odor when disturbed; often, simply standing next to a plant in the hot sun is unpleasant, and walking through the leaves results in smelly shoes and clothing. This characteristic gives the plant one of its common names, stinking gourd.

LEAVES: Large, coarse leaves shaped like an elongated heart grow alternately on long petioles (stemlets). Leaves are grayish-green above, and slightly paler below with prominent veins. Edges are very coarsely toothed; leaves are up to 12 inches long and half as wide below the midpoint. The leaves tend to fold inward along the midline.

FRUIT: A pulpy, rounded fruit with a firm skin and numerous seeds (called a *pepo*). Immature fruits are smooth and deep green with pale longitudinal stripes and speckles, resembling a tiny watermelon; they are 3 to 4 inches across. They ripen to tan or yellowish, and may become more egg-shaped when ripe. The fruits are inedible; some sources report that they are mildly toxic.

SEASON: Large yellow flowers are produced from late spring throughout late summer; fruits follow and are green much of the summer, ripening to tan or yellowish in fall. Like many members of the pumpkin family, by the time the fruit is ripe, the leaves may be brown and shriveled, or gone entirely.

COMPARE: Melon loco (*Apodanthera undulata*) is a vine with similar fruits, but its leaves are shorter, wider and wavy-edged and its fruits remain green; in our area, it is found in scattered areas of southern New Mexico.

NOTES: American Indians used various parts of the plant as a laxative, to cure toothache or swelling, and to treat sores and other skin conditions.

green = key identification feature

Plant overview

Ripe fruit

TREE

ALTERNATE
LEAVES

LATE SUMMER
TO EARLY FALL

Russian Olive –OR– Oleaster   *Elaeagnus angustifolia*

HABITAT: An introduced plant, Russian olive is found in floodplain forests, irrigation ditches and grasslands. It also grows along railroad grades, roads and fencelines. It tolerates seasonal flooding, but also survives in areas that suffer occasional drought. Prefers sun, but will grow in dappled shade. It is most common from the plains through the foothills.

GROWTH: A small tree, sometimes appearing as a large shrub; up to 30 feet tall, often with a rounded, spreading crown. Branches are silvery when young, maturing to reddish brown; some have small thorns.

LEAVES: Lance-shaped leaves are grayish-green above; the undersides are whitish. They grow alternately and are generally 2 to 4 inches long and one-quarter as wide, with smooth margins and a well-defined midrib. Leaves are rough-textured on both sides.

FRUIT: Oval drupes, about ½ inch long with a single large stone, are yellow when ripe, and are covered with fine silvery scales. Fruits grow abundantly along the stems from short, scaly stemlets. The fruit, although somewhat dry, is usually sweet, and can be eaten raw, cooked to add to baked goods, or used for jam. It is quite astringent when underripe; on individual plants, it may remain too astringent to eat even when ripe.

SEASON: In spring, numerous tiny yellow flowers with a strong scent grow along the branches. Some enjoy the scent; others find it overpowering and sneeze-inducing. Fruits follow, ripening in late summer to early fall.

COMPARE: Silverberry (pg. 310) is a related plant, but it is a shrub rather than a tree; its fruits are somewhat smaller than those of Russian olive and are whitish with silvery scales, and its leaves are silvery and more rounded. Buffaloberry (pg. 182) is another related plant, but it is a shrub; its fruits are much smaller than those of Russian olive and fruits are red when ripe.

NOTES: Russian olive was widely planted during the 1800s in disturbed areas; it is good for stabilizing embankments. It is considered invasive in some areas because it shades out native understory plants and spreads rapidly, and is listed as a noxious weed in Colorado and New Mexico.

green = key identification feature

TENDER
LEAFY PLANT

ALTERNATE
LEAVES

MID TO
LATE SUMMER

False Toadflax
–OR– **Northern Comandra**

Geocaulon lividum

HABITAT: This native perennial is found in cool, moist woods with dappled shade, particularly spruce forests; it also grows in mossy areas and peat bogs, and can tolerate poor soil. It grows from the plains through sub-alpine elevations.

GROWTH: An erect, leafy plant, 4 to 12 inches in height, that often grows in small colonies. Stems are usually unbranched and often have a reddish tint. Although it is able to photosynthesize, it also uses suckers (shoots) to attach itself to the roots of other plants, stealing water and nutrients from them; bearberry (pg. 130), spruce and pine are often hosts.

LEAVES: Oval leaves with blunt tips, ¾ to 1¼ inches long and one-half as wide, grow alternately from the stems on short petioles (stemlets) that flow smoothly into the leaf. Leaves are light green with a dull, almost dusty appearance; they sometimes have yellow veins which are caused by a blister rust fungus that also affects lodgepole and ponderosa pine. Leaves often develop a reddish hue in late summer.

FRUIT: A juicy, bright orangish-red drupe, typically about ¼ inch across, grows singly on a short stemlet from a leaf axil; fruits often grow upright. Some sources report them as edible but with a bad flavor, while others recommend against eating the fruit. It is best to consider them inedible.

SEASON: Flowers appear all summer; fruits ripen in mid to late summer.

COMPARE: False toadflax plants resemble bastard toadflax (pg. 86), but bastard toadflax fruit is streaked red and green and it has a prominent crown. Bog blueberry (*Vaccinium uliginosum*) is also a similar-looking plant, but its fruits are blue.

NOTES: False toadflax was used medicinally by American Indian peoples, who dressed wounds with a poultice made from the leaves and stems; the leaves and bark were also used to make a purgative tea. Some sources list false toadflax as *Comandra livida*.

green = key identification feature

TENDER
PLANT

ALTERNATE
LEAVES

MID TO
LATE SUMMER

Pinesap

Monotropa hypopithys

HABITAT: This unusual-looking native plant inhabits rich, shady coniferous woodlands, and is sometimes found along streams. It grows from the foothills through the sub-alpine zone.

GROWTH: Also called false beechdrops or yellow bird's-nest, pinesap does not synthesize sunlight to produce chlorophyll; instead, it gets its nutrients from fungi that, in turn, survive by extracting nutrients from trees and other plants (this relationship is called mycoheterotrophy). Pinesap is a delicate, waxy-looking plant that grows in clusters; individual stems are thick and fleshy, and are 2 to 11½ inches high. Bell-shaped flowers grow from upper parts of the plant, which arches down at the top while in flower. Stems, flowers and fruits are generally orangish to reddish, but may also be waxy white or yellowish, particularly early in the season.

LEAVES: Scale-like bracts (leaf-like structures) grow alternately, pressed against the stem; they may be the same color as, or darker than, the stem.

FRUIT: Rounded capsules about ¼ inch across grow upright, surrounded by floral remnants that clasp the base of the fruit; the stem also straightens to upright after flowering. Depending on stem color, the fruits may be orangish, yellowish, reddish or cream-colored. They are not edible.

SEASON: Pinesap produces flowers from mid to late summer, generally after a rain. Fruits follow, ripening throughout the season; they eventually dry out and split open to release their seeds.

COMPARE: Several other plants that don't produce chlorophyll grow in our area. Indian pipe (*M. uniflora*) is closely related to pinesap, but it has white stems and only a single, brownish fruit; in our area, Indian pipe is found in northern Idaho and parts of western Montana. Alpine cancer-root (pg. 302) is also similar, but its fruits are packed closely together and are whitish rather than orange. Woodland pinedrops (pg. 112) is much taller; it has hanging reddish fruits that are shaped like squat pumpkins.

NOTES: The genus name, *Monotropa*, is Greek for "one turn" and refers to the arching nature of the stem when flowering.

green = key identification feature

WOODY
VINE

ALTERNATE
LEAVES

LATE SUMMER
TO FALL

American Bittersweet

Celastrus scandens

HABITAT: Found in rich woods, swamp edges, field edges, ravines and disturbed areas; also grows on bluffs and rocky slopes. Bittersweet grows best and produces more fruit in full sun, but will tolerate light shade. It is uncommon in our area, and is most likely to be found in the plains zone.

GROWTH: A native perennial woody vine, bittersweet is typically seen climbing on trees, shrubs and fences; it has no tendrils and climbs by twisting around the supporting plant or structure. It can grow to 30 feet in length. Bark of older stems becomes scaly and corky in appearance.

LEAVES: The glossy, dark green leaves have finely serrated edges and are roughly oval in shape with sharply pointed tips; they are 2 to 4 inches long and one-half as wide. Leaves have short petioles (stemlets) and grow alternately on the vine, which has a slightly twisting habit, sometimes causing the leaves to appear to rotate along the stem. Leaves turn yellow and drop off in fall.

FRUIT: A round berry-like capsule, about ¼ inch across. Small clusters of fruits grow at the branch tips; fruits are green when young, ripening to orangish in late summer. In fall, the capsules split open and the shells fold backwards to reveal the bright, shiny orange-red seeds, making an attractive fall display. The fruits are mildly toxic and should not be eaten.

SEASON: The vine flowers in late spring. Unripe fruits develop in early summer, maturing in late summer and splitting open in fall.

COMPARE: Asiatic bittersweet (*C. orbiculatus*) is a non-native vine with similar orangish fruits; its leaves are almost round, and its fruits grow from leaf axils rather than from branch tips. Fortunately, Asiatic bittersweet does not (yet) grow in the wild in the western U.S.; it is an aggressive vine that kills other plants by smothering or girdling them. Although it is an attractive vine that is often sold at nurseries, it should not be planted as an ornamental due to the possibility of it escaping into the wild.

NOTES: The fruits remain on the plants through winter, providing food for grouse, pheasants, quail, rabbits, songbirds and squirrels.

green = key identification feature

Split capsule

SMALL
WOODY SHRUB

ALTERNATE
COMPOUND
LEAVES

LATE
SUMMER

Salmonberry

Rubus spectabilis

HABITAT: This native shrub grows in moist areas with dappled to moderate sun, including streambanks, edges and openings of coniferous wood-lands, ravines, scree fields and logged areas. Throughout its range, it grows at elevations from the plains through the foothills.

GROWTH: Salmonberries are brambles, sprawling vine-like shrubs that form thickets. Stems, called canes, grow to 13 feet in length and are generally upright but may also be arching. Young stems are greenish to reddish with fine hairs and small thorns; older stems are golden brown with papery, shreddy bark. Compared to raspberries and other *Rubus* species, salmonberry shrubs have a very leafy appearance.

LEAVES: Compound, doubly toothed leaves with sharply pointed tips grow alternately on the canes; leaves are bright green and generally wrinkly. Leaves have three leaflets; the central leaflet is up to 3 inches long and is shaped like a triangle with two rounded points. Side leaflets are shorter and have a shallow, small lobe on the edge farthest away from the central leaflet; together, the two side leaflets resemble the wings of a butterfly.

FRUIT: A compound drupe, up to ¾ inch across; a brush-like ring of hairs encircles the base of the fruit. Salmonberries typically grow singly, on a long stemlet. Ripe fruits are soft and typically orange, but may also be yellowish or red. Salmonberries detach easily from the plant, leaving the receptacle (core) behind, so the picked fruit is hollow. They are edible, but palatability varies from one plant to another; some are sweet, while others are tart or bland. There are no toxic look-alikes in our area.

SEASON: Large purple flowers appear in spring; fruits ripen in late summer.

COMPARE: Red raspberries (pg. 138) are related plants, but their fruits are rich red when ripe; their stems are prickly but have no thorns, and leaves on non-fruiting stems have five leaflets.

NOTES: Salmonberry grows only in a narrow band along the Pacific coast from southern Alaska to northwestern California, and in two Idaho counties (Bonner and Clearwater), but is often fairly common where it does grow.

green = key identification feature

TREE

ALTERNATE
COMPOUND
LEAVES

MID TO
LATE SUMMER

Western Soapberry

Sapindus saponaria

HABITAT: Well-drained areas such as edges of forests, fields and stream-banks; also found on canyon sides and in bottomlands, desert washes and arroyos. An adaptable tree that can tolerate infertile soil as well as wind, drought and heat. It grows from the plains through the foothills, and is common in semi-desert shrublands.

GROWTH: This native tree can grow to 50 feet in height, although it is usually much shorter; the crown is full, and some branches may bend low enough that the leaves almost touch the ground. The trunk has reddish-brown bark with raised, gray plates that fall off in large pieces. Soapberry produces suckers and may grow in colonies.

LEAVES: Compound leaves, 12 to 18 inches in length with 4 to 10 pairs of leaflets, grow alternately; a terminal leaflet is often present. Leaflets are 2 to 3 inches in length, with smooth edges and a sharply pointed tip; they are bright green, smooth and glossy above, paler and fuzzy below. Leaflets are asymmetrical; the half towards the branch tip is broader than the half closer to the trunk and the leaflet is usually deeply curved, resembling a crescent moon. Leaves turn yellow in fall.

FRUIT: Round orangish or golden-yellow drupes grow in branched racemes (long clusters of multiple fruits) at the tips of branches; as they ripen, the skin becomes wrinkled and translucent. Each fruit is ½ to ¾ inch across, and usually contains one dark-brown seed. Fruits often persist over winter, remaining on the tree through the next flowering cycle (as in the photo at right). The fruits contain saponin, a bitter substance that is toxic in large doses; they should not be eaten.

SEASON: Creamy yellow flowers profusely adorn the tree in late spring. Fruits follow, and ripen in mid to late summer.

COMPARE: Soapberry leaves resemble those of walnut (*Juglans* spp.) or hickory (*Carya* spp.), but hickory and walnut produce nuts, not drupes.

NOTES: The fruits contain saponin, a foaming compound that has been used as a soap substitute. It may cause an allergic reaction in some.

green = key identification feature

TREE

ALTERNATE
LEAVES

MID TO
LATE SUMMER

Apricot

Peach

Apricot –AND– Peach

Prunus spp.

HABITAT: Domestic apricots (*Prunus armeniaca*) or peaches (*P. persica*) are found occasionally in the wild. They may be survivors of gardens planted by farmers or homesteaders, or may have grown from a picnicker's discarded pit. Both do best in well-drained, moist soil and produce more fruit in sunny areas. They grow from the plains through the montane zones.

GROWTH: Both are small non-native trees, up to 25 feet tall with an open, rounded crown. Branches angle strongly upward, giving the plants a distinctive profile. Young stems are smooth and reddish to greenish, with prominent lenticels (breathing pores). Older bark is scaly and irregular; apricot bark tends to be dark brown, while peach bark is more reddish.

LEAVES: Both have finely toothed leaves that grow alternately. Apricot leaves are oval to heart-shaped, typically 2 to 3 inches long and two-thirds as wide; they have long petioles (stemlets) that are usually reddish. Peach leaves are distinctly narrow, 3 to 6 inches long and one-third to one-quarter as wide, with short greenish petioles; leaves often curve backwards, folding along the midrib.

FRUIT: Both are rounded drupes with fuzzy skin; the fruits have a noticeable cleft and a large, pitted stone. Wild apricots are usually 1 inch across or smaller with pale yellowish-orange skin; peaches are 1 to 2 inches across and are usually yellowish with a reddish blush, although wild peaches may be lighter in color than domestic peaches. With both species, flavor varies from tree to tree; some are very sweet, while others are tart or slightly bitter. All are edible; there are no toxic look-alikes. The leaves, twigs and seeds of both contain toxins and should not be eaten.

SEASON: Both flower in early spring; fruits are ripe in mid to late summer.

COMPARE: American wild plums (pg. 186) have similar but shorter leaves; their fruits are reddish-orange with a dusty bloom, but are smooth-skinned rather than fuzzy.

NOTES: When sweet wild apricots or peaches are found, they are excellent eaten out-of-hand. Tart or slightly bitter fruits work well for pickling.

green = key identification feature

Apricot

Peach

TREE

ALTERNATE
COMPOUND
LEAVES

LATE SUMMER
THROUGH FALL

Greene's

European

Mountain Ash (several)

Sorbus spp.

HABITAT: Two varieties of mountain ash inhabit our area: the native Greene's mountain ash (*Sorbus scopulina*; also called Cascade or western mountain ash) and the introduced European mountain ash (*S. aucuparia*). They are found on rocky ridges, in sun-dappled woods, and at the edges of forests. They require ample moisture and moderate to full sunlight. Both grow from the plains through the montane zones.

GROWTH: Both are small trees with spreading branches and an open crown. Greene's is generally less than 16 feet tall and often has multiple trunks; European mountain ash may be **up to 40 feet tall** and typically has a single trunk. Bark of both is smooth and brownish with numerous lenticels (breathing pores) when young, turning rough and gray with age.

LEAVES: Compound leaves with 11 to 15 leaflets grow alternately on the stems. Leaves are up to 8 inches long overall; the leaflets have coarsely serrated edges and are paler below than above. Greene's mountain ash leaflets are **1 to 2½ inches long**, with **pointed tips**; European mountain ash leaflets are up to 1½ inches long, with **blunt tips**.

FRUIT: Small pomes, each about ⅜ inch across, grow in dense, flat-topped clusters. Fruits of both are greenish-white when immature, ripening to **reddish-orange**. It can be difficult to distinguish between species when confronted with them in the field; fortunately, fruits from both are edible. The fruit is somewhat astringent, becoming a bit milder after a frost. It is often used to make jelly, or as a seasoning for meat.

SEASON: Fruits ripen in late summer through fall, and remain on the trees through winter.

COMPARE: The native American mountain ash (*S. americana*) is found east of the Mississippi River but not in our area; its leaves are narrower, and its ripe fruits are deep orange.

NOTES: Mountain ash is an important fall and winter food source for birds, including grouse, waxwings and grosbeaks, as well as for black bears.

green = key identification feature

Greene's mountain ash

EDIBLE

TENDER
LEAFY PLANT

ALTERNATE
COMPOUND
LEAVES

EARLY
SUMMER

Ground-Plum Milkvetch

Astragalus crassicarpus

HABITAT: This native perennial grows in open, rocky or gravelly areas, including rocky meadows and prairies, along roadsides, and in sparse, rocky woodlands. It grows in the plains zone.

GROWTH: Stems grow from a central crown, and are typically 6 to 12 inches in length, although they may be longer. Stems are fleshy and covered with fine hairs; they are reddish, or green tinged with red. Young stems are upright, but when fruits develop, the stems usually sprawl on the ground. In late spring, the plants have abundant clusters of orchid-like flowers that are whitish, pink or purplish. Ground-plum have no tendrils.

LEAVES: Compound leaves, 2 to 5 inches in length, grow alternately. Leaves have seven to 16 pairs of small, narrow, lance-shaped leaflets on the hairy, pale-green leaf stemlet; a terminal leaflet is usually present. Leaflets are pale and dull green in color, with smooth edges; they average ¾ inch in length and are about one-quarter as wide. Undersides are hairy; the top sides may be smooth, or have scattered fine hairs.

FRUIT: Plump, smooth-skinned, egg-shaped pods, about 1 inch long and containing numerous small black seeds, grow in clusters at the ends of non-leafy stems. Fruits are greenish when immature, ripening to brickish-red. They have two lengthwise seams; the bottom of the fruit bears a long, thin tail. Young fruits are edible raw, cooked or pickled; care must be taken to ensure proper identification, as some plants with similar leaves and flowers have toxic fruits (see below). Older fruits are not considered edible.

SEASON: Fruits develop in late spring, ripening in early summer.

COMPARE: Numerous other plants with similar leaves and flowers inhabit our area; some have similar fruits, while others have fruits that are shaped like pea pods or large kidney beans. These include other *Astragalus*; purple locoweed (*Oxytropis lambertii*); and numerous vetches (*Vicia* spp.), which are vining plants with tendrils. Many of these pea pod-like or oval fruits are toxic; none should be eaten.

NOTES: Seek advice from a skilled forager before eating ground-plum.

green = key identification feature

TENDER
LEAFY PLANT

SINGLE
COMPOUND
LEAF

SUMMER

*see below

Strawberries (several)

Fragaria spp.

HABITAT: Strawberries grow best in well-drained soil with full sun to part shade, and are often found in rocky areas alongside rural roads, streams and lakes; they also grow in open woodlands, disturbed areas, meadows and fields. They grow from the plains through the sub-alpine zones.

GROWTH: Two types of native wild strawberries inhabit our region: the wild or Virginia strawberry (*Fragaria virginiana*), and the woodland strawberry (*F. vesca*). Both are erect, leafy plants 4 to 8 inches high, with white, 5-petaled flowers. Since both types spread by runners (horizontal stems), it's not uncommon to find a good-sized patch of wild strawberries.

LEAVES: A single coarsely toothed, three-part leaf grows at the end of a long, fuzzy stem. Leaves of woodland strawberry are bright green with prominent veins; those of Virginia strawberry are dull green with shallow veins (Al Schneider, Southwest Colorado Wildflowers). The terminal tooth of a woodland strawberry leaf is longer than the surrounding teeth, while it is shorter than the surrounding teeth on a Virginia strawberry.

FRUIT: The heart-shaped strawberry is technically not a fruit; the actual fruits are the seeds on the surface of the swollen receptacle (the base of the flower, which is normally inside the fruit). Woodland strawberries are about ½ inch long when mature; the seeds sit on the surface. Virginia strawberries are slightly smaller, and the seeds are slightly embedded in depressions on the surface. Both fruits are rich red when ripe. Strawberries flower throughout summer, so flowers and fruit are present at the same time once the season starts. There are no toxic look-alikes.

SEASON: Strawberries flower from late spring through early fall; tiny yellow fruits follow the flowers, swelling and ripening to a juicy red fruit a week or two later. Strawberries often produce fruit all summer.

COMPARE: The dwarf red raspberry (pg. 140) has similar trifoliate leaves and red fruit, but the fruit is a compound drupe.

NOTES: Although smaller than commercial varieties, wild strawberries are sweeter and more intensely flavored, and well worth seeking.

green = key identification feature

*combined range

Virginia strawberry

Woodland strawberry

TENDER
LEAFY PLANT

ALTERNATE
LEAVES

SUMMER

Bastard Toadflax

Comandra umbellata

HABITAT: Meadows, grasslands, washes, high hillsides, woodland edges, and dry, open woods; occasionally found in mixed conifer forests. It requires plenty of sunlight and good drainage. It grows from the plains through the montane zones, and is also found in semi-desert shrublands.

GROWTH: An erect native perennial, typically less than 8 inches tall. It grows from rhizomes (underground root-bearing stems), often in large colonies. Stems are light green and smooth, and woody near the base. Although it is able to photosynthesize, it also uses suckers (shoots) to attach itself to the roots of other plants, stealing water and nutrients from them.

LEAVES: The thick, alternate leaves are 1 to 2 inches long and about one-quarter as wide. They are attached directly to the stem or by a very short petiole (stemlet). Leaves are light grayish-green and smooth, with smooth edges; some leaf tips may have a slight reddish tinge. The mid-vein is prominent on the underside of the leaf.

FRUIT: The rounded drupes about ¼ inch across are reddish with green streaks or blotches and a long, pinkish or whitish floral crown at the end; the fruits seem large in proportion to the plant. Fruits grow on long stemlets in clusters at the end of the main stem. The fruits are sweet when young, but have thin flesh with a slightly oily texture. They make a fairly decent trailside nibble, but are not worth seeking out. Later in the season, the fruits turn brown and become unappetizing.

SEASON: Bastard toadflax produces white flowers in late spring through midsummer; fruits ripen throughout the summer.

COMPARE: The leaves and growth habit of bastard toadflax resemble true toadflax (*Linaria* spp.), but *Linaria* don't produce drupes. False toadflax (pg. 68) is similar, but its ripe fruits are bright orange and have no crown.

NOTES: Flower stamens have small hairs at their bases, giving the plant its species name, *Comandra* (a combination of the Greek words for "hair" and "man"). *Umbellata* refers to the flat-topped, umbrella-like flower clusters. Comandra is an alternate common name for bastard toadflax.

green = key identification feature

TENDER
LEAFY PLANT

BASAL
LEAVES

SUMMER

*see below

Bladderpod (several)

Physaria and *Lesquerella* spp.

HABITAT: Bladderpods inhabit semi-desert areas from the plains through the alpine zones. There are two related groups of these native plants; both produce rubbery, hollow balloon-like fruits that are actually pods. Although multiple fruits grow closely together on each fruiting stalk, close examination reveals that each *Lesquerella* fruit is a single balloon-like pod, while each *Physaria* fruit consists of paired balloon-like pods (*Physaria* are commonly called double bladderpods or twinpods).

GROWTH: Bladderpods are short ground-hugging plants with a circle of basal leaves. Flowers, followed by fruits, grow on stalks, usually 2 to 6 inches long, that either form a ring around the outside perimeter of the leaves or grow throughout the circle of leaves.

LEAVES: The most common single-fruit bladderpod in our area is alpine bladderpod (*L. alpina*); sharpleaf twinpod (*P. acutifolia*; pictured at right) is the most common double bladderpod. Leaves of alpine bladderpod are ½ to 1½ inches long and are lance-shaped, with a long, narrow base and rounded tip. Sharpleaf twinpod's leaves resemble a short-stemmed spoon, with a stubby neck and a broad cup at the end; they are up to 3½ inches long. Leaves of both species are silvery-green and hairy.

FRUIT: Inflated, spongy, somewhat lumpy pods that are generally ¾ inch long and covered with fine hairs grow in tight clusters on fruiting stalks. Ripe fruits range from yellow to pinkish to purplish. They are not edible.

SEASON: Bladderpods flower from spring through early summer; fruits ripen throughout summer.

COMPARE: Other bladderpods, both single and double, grow in various areas throughout our region; all are recognizable by the inflated fruits.

NOTES: Some plant authorities have recently combined the *Lesquerella* group with the *Physaria* group due to the botanical similarities between the plants (*Novon* 12, 2002: Missouri Botanical Garden); as an example, in this new naming convention *L. alpina* would be called *P. reediana*.

green = key identification feature

*combined range

TENDER
LEAFY PLANT

COMPOUND
LEAVES

SUMMER

Red Baneberry

Actaea rubra

HABITAT: This native plant grows in shady areas of moist hardwoods and mixed-wood forests; it often grows alongside streams and may be found in areas that flood seasonally. It is found from the plains through the sub-alpine zones.

GROWTH: Two to four doubly compound leaves, each up to 15 inches long, grow alternately on the main stem. The total height is 1 to 2½ feet. Flowers grow on a separate, leafless stalk that branches off one of the leaf stalks and generally rise above the surrounding leaves.

LEAVES: Three large compound leaflets grow on each of the long leaf stalks attached to the main stem; each has three or five smooth, sharply toothed leaflets oppositely attached by short stalks. The terminal leaflet is often slightly larger than side leaflets.

FRUIT: Firm, glossy berries about ⅜ inch long, slightly oval to round with a shallow vertical groove. Each berry has a small black dot at the bottom. Berries are typically red, although sometimes they are white. Berries grow in a cluster at the top of the thin flower stalk, and are attached to the stalk by thin, green stemlets. The berries are toxic.

SEASON: Ripe berries can be seen throughout the summer.

COMPARE: The related white baneberry (*A. pachypoda*) has similar leaves, but the flower stalk and stemlets are thick and knobby, usually reddish-pink, while those of the red baneberry are green and thin; the dot on the bottom of the berry is larger on white baneberries. White baneberry does not grow in our area; it is found in the eastern U.S. and the central plains states.

NOTES: All parts of the plant should be considered toxic; contact with leaves may cause skin irritation in sensitive individuals. Ingestion of the berries may lead to dizziness, vomiting or cardiac arrest; children are especially susceptible. Birds eat the berries with no ill effect, helping disperse the seeds. The white-berried form is sometimes referred to as "doll's eyes" due to the appearance of the black spots against the smooth, glossy white berries.

green = key identification feature

Red baneberry
with white berries

TENDER
LEAFY PLANT

ALTERNATE
LEAVES

MID TO
LATE SUMMER

Strawberry Spinach

Chenopodium capitatum

HABITAT: This native annual is found in sunny, well-drained areas, including forest clearings and edges, open valleys, along trails and roads, and on waste ground; it is one of the first plants to appear after a forest fire. It grows from the foothills through the lower parts of the alpine zone.

GROWTH: Sturdy, ridged stems grow to a height of 1 to 2 feet from a central taproot; an individual plant may have many stems that fan out to a foot or more in width. The stems and leaves turn red in late summer. The large taproots can be eaten raw, or boiled as a cooked vegetable.

LEAVES: Broad, smooth triangular-shaped leaves, typically 1 to 2 inches long and two-thirds as wide near the base, grow alternately on long petioles (stemlets). Leaf edges usually have large teeth, or may appear wavy; often, the two teeth nearest the base are longer and narrower, appearing ear-like. The leaves are edible raw, or cooked like spinach.

FRUIT: The "fruit" is actually a tight, globular cluster of tiny, bright red flowers. The clusters grow in leaf axils and along the upper stem; they are green at first, turning deep red as they mature. When red, they look a bit like raspberries that are adhering to the stem. Although very seedy, fully red clusters are juicy and edible, with a taste like mild, slightly sweet cauliflower; they make an interesting trail nibble, and are often used in salads. There are no toxic look-alikes with similar growth habits.

SEASON: Flower clusters are green in early summer, turning red from mid to late summer.

COMPARE: Other members of the *Chenopodium* family have similar leaves and growth habits, but the flower clusters do not turn red.

NOTES: This plant has many common names, including beetberry, Indian paint and strawberry blite. The word "blite" comes from the Latin word *blitum*, which refers to a spinach-like plant with edible leaves; another explanation is that blite is a corruption of "blight," a reference to the fruit, which looks like an unnatural growth. *Chenopodium* is Greek for "goose foot," a reference to the leaf shape; *capitatum* means "with a head."

green = key identification feature

TENDER
PLANT

MID TO
LATE SUMMER

Spotted

Striped, Spring
*see below

Coralroot (several)

Corallorhiza spp.

HABITAT: Four varieties of this native orchid with red fruits grow in our area. Spotted coralroot (*Corallorhiza maculata*) is the most common; it inhabits shaded coniferous forests at all elevations through the sub-alpine zone; also found on rocky slopes in the alpine zone. Striped coralroot (*C. striata*) inhabits damp woods and boggy areas through the montane zone. Spring coralroot (*C. wisteriana*) grows in openings in pine-aspen forests through the montane zone. Pacific coralroot (*C. mertensiana*) is uncommon, only found scattered in parts of Idaho, Wyoming and Montana, where it grows in moist coniferous and mixed-wood forests of the plains zone.

GROWTH: The orchids discussed here lack chlorophyll; they get their nutrients from fungi that, in turn, survive by extracting nutrients from trees and other plants (this relationship is called mycoheterotrophy). All have unbranched stems that are reddish, purplish or tan and average 20 inches tall. Numerous small flowers grow on the upper stem; they have thin, widely spread side petals and a distinct, rounded petal (called a lip) at the base. Subtle flower characteristics are used to distinguish between the various orchids; consult a good wildflower book for more details.

LEAVES: These plants have sheath-like leaves rather than regular leaves.

FRUIT: The fruits of the orchids discussed here are very similar, and it is very difficult to know which orchid you've found if the plant is not flowering. All are oblong, smooth reddish capsules, ½ to 1 inch long and one-third as wide, hanging from their stemlets; capsules of striped coralroot have subtle stripes, while the others are solid-colored. The fruits are not edible.

SEASON: These orchids bloom from spring through summer; fruits are present in mid to late summer.

COMPARE: Yellow coralroot (*C. trifida*) is similar, but its stems, flowers and fruits are greenish-yellow. Please also see the text on pg. 70 for information about other similar plants that don't produce chlorophyll.

NOTES: These orchids are fragile plants that should never be disturbed; some are protected due to their rarity.

green = key identification feature

*combined range

TENDER
LEAFY PLANT

ALTERNATE
LEAVES

MID TO
LATE SUMMER

Asparagus

Asparagus officinalis

HABITAT: This escapee from cultivation is found in sunny pastures, fields, roadsides and ditches, and along fencerows, embankments and railroad grades, especially those near agricultural areas. It grows in the plains zone.

GROWTH: Asparagus is a commonly grown vegetable that develops into a bushy, multi-stemmed fern-like plant with **feathery, drooping fronds**. It can grow up to 6 feet in height, with equal width. In midsummer, small berries develop on the fronds.

LEAVES: The true leaves are actually **small scales on the main stem**; they are the same as the dark, dagger-like leaves on the stalk of the familiar asparagus spear. The wispy, fern-like appearance of the plant comes from branches with soft, needle-like leaves; the branches grow alternately on the main stem.

FRUIT: Round red berries, about ¼ inch across or slightly larger, grow on thin, bent stemlets from the upper wispy branches. The berries contain toxins and should not be eaten.

SEASON: Asparagus shoots develop into the "asparagus fern" by early summer. Berries soon develop; they are green at first, ripening to red by mid to late summer.

COMPARE: Asparagus is easy to identify at all stages. At a distance, the fern stage of the plant may resemble any number of overgrown leafy plants, but close inspection of an asparagus plant, with its scale-like leaves on the stalks, will confirm its identity. Check the base of the plant; you'll see the asparagus spears you're familiar with, but the pointy top has grown into the fern-like stems. You may even be able to see last year's withered, browned stalks (see small photo at right). Remember the location, and come back the following spring to harvest fresh, wild-grown asparagus spears.

NOTES: Wild asparagus is simply the cultivated vegetable that has escaped the farm or garden. Birds eat the red berries, and the wild plants are often found near farms that grow asparagus.

green = key identification feature

Closeup of base

Asparagus plant in "fern stage"

TENDER
LEAFY PLANT

WHORLED
LEAVES

MID TO
LATE SUMMER

Bunchberry

Cornus canadensis

HABITAT: This native plant inhabits cool, shady coniferous and mixed-wood forests; it is also sometimes found in boggy or swampy areas. It grows from the plains through the sub-alpine zones.

GROWTH: Technically a shrub, bunchberry grows as a leafy plant that is typically 4 to 8 inches high. It grows from a spreading underground rhizome (root-bearing stem) and is often found in a large colony.

LEAVES: Each plant has one or two groupings of four to six leaves that grow oppositely; pairs grow so closely spaced on the stem that the leaf groups have a whorled appearance. The deep green, shiny leaves are oval, with pointed ends and deep veins that curve from base to tip; they are typically 1 to 3 inches in length, and about three-quarters as wide. A flower stalk rises from the center of the top leaf pair.

FRUIT: Round, bright red drupes, ¼ inch across, grow in a cluster from the flower stalk at the top of the plant. The fruits are edible, but mealy and bland with hard seeds, and are not worth seeking out. They can be eaten raw as a trail nibble, or cooked into jam, jelly, sauce or pudding. Bunchberry is a good survival food to know about.

SEASON: Tiny greenish flowers with large white bracts (leaf-like structures) appear from late spring through early summer; the flowers develop into fruits, which ripen in mid to late summer.

COMPARE: Rough-fruited fairybells (pg. 100) has similar leaves, but they grow alternately along a long, zigzag stem; the fruits are larger and grow singly or in pairs rather than in a cluster.

NOTES: Bunchberries have a unique pollination method; when the closed flower is touched, it opens explosively—in less than a millisecond—to release its pollen, throwing it up to an inch away at a speed of 10 feet per second (according to a study reported in a 2005 edition of the journal *Nature*).

green = key identification feature

TENDER
LEAFY PLANT

ALTERNATE
LEAVES

MID TO
LATE SUMMER

Rough-Fruited Fairybells

Prosartes trachycarpa

HABITAT: This native plant is found in rich, shady areas with adequate moisture, such as streambanks and sun-dappled woodlands; it inhabits deciduous and coniferous forests. It grows from the plains through the sub-alpine zones.

GROWTH: Perennial, 12 to 24 inches high; stems typically fork several times. The stems are round and fairly thick; they are greenish, tan or reddish, and slightly downy. Stems may bend slightly at each leaf axil in zigzag fashion.

LEAVES: Heart-shaped to oval leaves grow alternately; they are attached directly to the stem, often in a clasping fashion. Leaves are typically 2 to 4 inches long and one-third as wide; they are broadest at the base, and have a sharp tip at the end. Distinct veins curve from the tip to the base; leaf edges are fringed with short hairs (visible with a lens).

FRUIT: One to three rounded, lumpy berries grow on short, fuzzy stemlets at the branch tips. They have velvety-textured or slightly warty skin, accounting for the common name. Immature fruits are small and green with three lobes, enlarging and becoming more round as they mature. The enlarged, rounded fruits turn orange before ripening to rich red; ripe berries are generally about ½ inch across. They are edible but tasteless. There are no toxic look-alikes that have the same rough-skinned texture.

SEASON: Small whitish bell-shaped flowers appear from spring through midsummer, growing on short stemlets at the branch tips. Fruits follow, and are ripe from mid through late summer.

COMPARE: Drops-of-gold or Hooker's fairybells (*P. hookeri*) is very similar, but its fruits are smooth-skinned; in our area, it is found in much of northern Idaho and in a few Montana counties. Clasping-leaved twisted-stalk (pg. 102) has similar stems and leaves, but its berries grow from leaf axils, on bent stemlets, all along the stem rather than just at the tip.

NOTES: Some sources list this plant as *Disporum trachycarpum*; drops-of-gold would then be listed as *D. hookeri*.

green = key identification feature

Immature fruits

Mature fruit

TENDER
LEAFY PLANT

ALTERNATE
LEAVES

LATE
SUMMER

Clasping-Leaved Twisted-Stalk

Streptopus amplexifolius

HABITAT: This native plant grows in moist, shady areas such as sun-dappled woodlands, streambanks and thickets; it inhabits both deciduous and coniferous forests. It grows from the plains through the sub-alpine zones.

GROWTH: Perennial, 1½ to 4½ feet high; plants will be tallest in moist, tangled areas. The stems are round and somewhat wiry; they are greenish and may have scattered small hairs near the base. Stems typically **fork several times**, and usually bend slightly at each leaf axil in zigzag fashion.

LEAVES: Lance-shaped to oval leaves grow alternately; they are attached directly to the stem in a **clasping** fashion. Leaves are 2 to 5½ inches long and one-half to one-third as wide; they are broadest at the base, and have a sharp tip at the end. Distinct veins curve from the base to the tip.

FRUIT: Juicy, oblong red berries about ½ inch long grow singly or in pairs at the leaf axils. Berries hang **below the leaves** on a **thin stemlet that has a noticeable bend or twist in it**; it is this "twisted" stemlet that gives the plant its common name. Many sources say that twisted-stalk berries are edible but may cause diarrhea if more than a few are eaten; other sources list them as mildly toxic. It's best to consider them inedible.

SEASON: Small whitish bell-shaped flowers appear in midsummer. Fruits follow, and are ripe in late summer.

COMPARE: Several plants in our area have very similar stems and leaves; here are key points to distinguish them from clasping-leaved twisted-stalk. Rough-fruited fairybells (pg. 100) bears fruits at the end of the stem rather than along the stems; it is also a shorter plant. Stems of common false Solomon's seal (pg. 104) do not fork, and the plant bears large clusters of tiny berries at the tip of the stem. Stems of small twisted-stalk (*S. streptopoides*) do not fork and the plant is less than 8 inches tall; in our area, it grows only in northern Idaho.

NOTES: Some sources list the scientific name for this plant as *S. fassettii*.

green = key identification feature

Overview of plant

Berry stemlet, clasping leaf base

TENDER
LEAFY PLANT

ALTERNATE
LEAVES

LATE
SUMMER

Common False Solomon's Seal

Maianthemum racemosum

HABITAT: This native plant is common and widespread in moist deciduous or mixed-wood forests from the plains through sub-alpine elevations.

GROWTH: The single stem usually grows in zigzag fashion, bending slightly at each leaf axil; it is up to 3 feet long. The plant is upright when young, but as it matures, it reclines until it is almost horizontal. Plants grow from rhizomes (underground root-bearing stems) and often form colonies.

LEAVES: Bright green, shiny leaves are lance-shaped, with a sharp tip at the end; they are up to 8 inches long and about one-third as wide. Leaves are attached directly to the stem in an alternate arrangement, and feature deep parallel veins curving from base to tip.

FRUIT: Smooth, round berries grow in a long cluster at the end of the stem; each berry is about ⅛ inch across. Unripe berries are greenish with tiny purple blotches; ripe berries are deep red. The berries are bittersweet and generally regarded as inedible, although ripe berries may have been eaten by American Indians in the past (Sam Thayer).

SEASON: Unripe berries are present from late spring through midsummer; berries turn pinkish with red spots before ripening fully in late summer.

COMPARE: Clasping-leaved twisted-stalk (pg. 102) has similar leaves, but it is a branching plant and its fruits grow from leaf axils. Starry false Solomon's seal (pg. 106) has a cluster of red fruits at the end of the stem, but the plant is shorter and the leaves are narrower; it tends to be more upright rather than reclining, and the fruits are pumpkin-shaped. Smooth Solomon's seal (pg. 220) bears fruit at the leaf axils rather than at the end of the stem; fruits are blue. False lily of the valley (*M. dilatatum*) is a related plant, but individual stems have only 1 to 3 leaves, which are broad and heart-shaped; in our area, it grows only in a few Idaho counties.

NOTES: This plant is also called feathery false lily of the valley. Some texts list it as *Smilacina racemosa* or *M. amplexicaule*.

green = key identification feature

Unripe berries

TENDER
LEAFY PLANT

ALTERNATE
LEAVES

LATE
SUMMER

Starry False Solomon's Seal *Maianthemum stellatum*

HABITAT: This native perennial inhabits cool, moist forests; it grows adjacent to streams, and is also found in sandy areas near marshes. Starry false Solomon's seal is often one of the first plants to grow after a forest fire. It grows from the plains through the sub-alpine zones.

GROWTH: The single stem usually grows in a zigzag fashion, bending slightly at each leaf axil; it is up to 2 feet in length. The stems arch some-what, but the plant is not droopy. Plants grow from rhizomes (underground root-bearing stems) and often form colonies.

LEAVES: Lance-shaped leaves, up to 6 inches long and one-quarter as wide, grow alternately from the main stem, which typically bends slightly at each leaf axil. Leaves attach directly to the stem, and are stiff and bluish-green, with prominent parallel veins; they are smooth on top and may be slightly hairy underneath.

FRUIT: A short raceme (a cluster of multiple fruits) of berries grows at the end of the stem. Unripe berries are green with maroon stripes, and are shaped like a small, squat pumpkin about 5/16 inch across. The berries turn yellowish, then ripen to dark red with pale specks before turning solid red. Ripe berries are edible raw or cooked, but have a laxative effect if eaten raw. They have a bittersweet flavor, and are reportedly high in vitamin C.

SEASON: Star-shaped white flowers, which give the plant its common name, appear from mid spring to early summer. The green berries follow, ripening to red by late summer.

COMPARE: Please see the discussion of similar plants listed in common false Solomon's seal on pg. 104. Starry false Solomon's seal is most likely to be confused with common false Solomon's seal. Common false Solomon's seal is generally a larger plant, with more leaves and a larger number of berries in the terminal cluster; also, its berries are tiny and round, and are greenish speckled with purple when unripe.

NOTES: Starry false Solomon's seal is sometimes listed in references as *Smilacina stellata*. Ruffed grouse eat the ripe berries in autumn.

green = key identification feature

Unripe berries

TENDER
LEAFY PLANT

BASAL
LEAVES

LATE
SUMMER

*see below

Pyrola Wintergreen (several)

Pyrola spp.

HABITAT: Five species of *Pyrola* wintergreen are found in our area. All inhabit moist, shady woodlands. Green wintergreen (*Pyrola chlorantha*), pink wintergreen (*P. asarifolia* ssp. *bracteata*), liverleaf wintergreen (*P. asarifolia* ssp. *asarifolia*) and lesser wintergreen (*P. minor*; also called snowline wintergreen) are found from the foothills through the sub-alpine zones. White-veined wintergreen (*P. picta*) grows from the foothills through the montane zones; shinleaf (*P. elliptica*) is found only at plains elevations.

GROWTH: The wintergreen species discussed here are native perennials. Upright, unbranched stems grow from a ground-hugging cluster of leaves or occasionally directly from bare ground with no leaves; cup-shaped flowers hang down on short stemlets from the upper parts of the stems, developing into berry-like capsules. White-veined and pink wintergreen may get to 15 inches in height but are usually shorter. Shinleaf and green wintergreen are up to 10 inches tall; lesser wintergreen is 6 inches or shorter.

LEAVES: All *Pyrola* leaves have petioles (stemlets) and grow basally; veins on the top surface are generally paler than the leaf. Green and lesser wintergreen leaves are nearly round and up to 1⅛ inches long; green wintergreen's petiole is often longer than the leaf, while it is shorter than the leaf on lesser wintergreen. Pink wintergreen leaves are oval with a softly pointed tip; they are up to 2½ inches long. Shinleaf and white-veined leaves are oval to egg-shaped and up to 3¼ inches long; veins of white-veined wintergreen are white with a wide white margin.

FRUIT: Rounded, 5-chambered capsules about ¼ inch across with a long, thin floral remnant on the base are green when immature, hanging down on short stemlets. The capsules gradually turn pinkish-red; when fully mature, they stand upright. The fruits are not edible.

SEASON: Fruits ripen in late summer. Leaves remain green all year.

COMPARE: Alpine spicy wintergreen (pg. 122) is botanically related, but it is a vining plant whose fruits are berries that grow on short stemlets.

NOTES: *Pyrola* contain aspirin-like compounds, and are used medicinally.

green = key identification feature   *combined range

Green wintergreen

Upright capsules

TENDER
LEAFY PLANT

ALTERNATE
LEAVES
(TYP.)

SUMMER
THROUGH
EARLY FALL

Rough Menodora –OR– Twinberry *Menodora scabra*

HABITAT: This native perennial inhabits sandy, sun-drenched areas, including brushy deserts, grasslands, meadows, rocky slopes, dry hillsides, roadsides, and woodlands with pinyon pine and scrub oak. It tolerates high heat and dry conditions and is found in the plains and foothills zones; it also grows in semi-desert shrublands.

GROWTH: Menodora grows in a clump that can appear scrubby and open, or fairly full; clumps can be up to 3 feet across. Numerous round, rough-textured stems, up to 2 feet in height, grow upright from the center of the clump, spreading outward at the edges. Leaves are small and sparse, so the plant appears to be mostly stems. Bright yellow 5-lobed flowers grow at the ends of the stems from late spring through late summer.

LEAVES: Lance-shaped leaves with smooth edges are attached directly to the stems; at the base of the plant, leaves grow oppositely, but the leaves on the remainder of the long stems are attached alternately. They are ⅓ to 1⅛ inches long, and less than one-quarter as wide. The midvein is prominent on both surfaces.

FRUIT: A smooth capsule with two rounded, ball-like lobes replaces each flower. Each lobe is about ¼ inch across, and is surrounded by green, spiky sepals (leaf-like petals). The fruits are greenish at first, developing a reddish blush before ripening to deep red; they eventually dry out and turn tan before splitting open to disperse their seeds. The fruits are not edible.

SEASON: Fruits develop throughout the summer and into early fall, and are present on the plants at the same time as the yellow flowers.

COMPARE: The lanky stems and small, narrow leaves resemble other desert plants, including pearly everlasting (*Anaphalis margaritacea*); however, the red, two-lobed fruits of rough menodora make it easy to identify.

NOTES: When rough menodora is fruiting, the clump appears to be covered with paired, glossy red balls, giving it the common name of frog's eyes.

green = key identification feature

Ripe fruit

TENDER
PLANT

ALTERNATE
LEAVES

MIDSUMMER
TO EARLY
FALL

Woodland Pinedrops

Pterospora andromedea

HABITAT: This native perennial is most common in rich, shady coniferous forests, although it also grows in mixed-wood forests. It is found from the plains through the sub-alpine zones.

GROWTH: Woodland pinedrops does not synthesize sunlight to produce chlorophyll; instead, it gets its nutrients from fungi that, in turn, survive by extracting nutrients from trees and other plants (this relationship is called mycoheterotrophy). It grows as an unbranched stem, either singly or in clusters; the stem is reddish and covered with fine, white hairs that secrete a sticky substance. When young and beginning to flower, the stem is less than a foot in height; as it matures, it grows rapidly and is typically about 3 feet tall when fully mature. The flower buds, which look like whitish berries, grow at the tip in a tight, spiraling cluster; buds at the bottom of the stem open first. The bell-shaped flowers are cream-colored or pinkish and waxy-looking; they hang from drooping, downy stemlets that are red.

LEAVES: Thin bracts (leaf-like structures) grow alternately on the lower part of the stem; on young plants, they are about 1 inch long and ⅛ inch wide, and the tips curl away from the stem. As the plant matures, the tips of the bracts shrivel until all that remains are wedge-shaped scales.

FRUIT: Capsules about ½ inch across and ⅓ inch deep hang from the drooping red floral stemlets. They are composed of pillowy-looking segments and look like tiny, squat pumpkins. Fully developed fruits are typically reddish, but may also appear orangish or yellowish with a reddish blush; as they age, they turn brown and split open to scatter tiny seeds that have translucent, skirt-like wings. The fruits are not edible.

SEASON: Pinedrops flower from mid through late summer; ripe fruits are present from midsummer to early fall. Dried fruits persist into winter.

COMPARE: Please see the text on pg. 70 for information about other similar plants that don't produce chlorophyll.

NOTES: This plant also goes by the curious name of yellow bird's nest.

green = key identification feature

Fully developed fruits

Buds and flowers

CACTUS

MID TO
LATE SUMMER

Claret cup

Nylon
hedgehog

Hedgehog Cacti (several)

Echinocereus spp.

HABITAT: Two native varieties of this cactus family are found in all of the southern states in our area, and ten more varieties are found in at least one of them. Claret cup (*Echinocereus triglochidiatus*; also called kingcup hedgehog cactus) and nylon hedgehog cactus (*E. coccineus*) are found in grasslands, rocky or gravelly areas and open pinyon-juniper woodlands; also found on sagebrush flats. They grow in the foothills and semi-desert shrublands zones, and may also be found in montane forests.

GROWTH: Hedgehog cacti are *stem succulents*, non-woody plants that hold water in their soft tissue. Hedgehogs grow singly or in large, clustering mounds with dozens—even hundreds—of the cylindrical, fleshy stems. Individual stems of both species discussed here are up to 15 inches tall and one-quarter to one-half as wide; stems have 5 to 12 vertical ribs that are armed with up to 10 heavy spines radiating from *areoles*, rounded tuft-like buds spaced evenly along the skin. Spines are ⅝ to 3 inches long. These two hedgehogs are difficult to tell apart when not in flower; claret cup tends to be slightly larger than nylon hedgehog.

LEAVES: No normal leaves; the spines may be considered modified leaves.

FRUIT: Egg-shaped berries, typically 1 to 1¼ inches long, grow on the upper parts of the stems; they are covered with spines that are smaller than those on the stems, and have a long, brown flower remnant at the end. The fruits are red when ripe, with whitish flesh and numerous small black seeds; they are juicy and sweet, and are edible raw or cooked once the spines have been removed (usually by burning off). Fruits are often made into jam; sliced fruits are sometimes baked with a heavy coat of sugar.

SEASON: Hedgehogs produce stunning red flowers in late spring to early summer; fruits develop over summer, ripening in mid to late summer.

COMPARE: The other hedgehogs in our area grow primarily in New Mexico. They have the same general appearance as the two cacti discussed here, but may be more or less spiny; overall plants may be smaller or larger.

NOTES: The flowers stay open 24 hours a day for a week or more.

green = key identification feature

Claret cup

CACTUS

MID TO
LATE SUMMER

*see below

Prickly Pear Cacti (several)

Opuntia spp.

HABITAT: A dozen native varieties of this jointed, flat-stemmed cactus grow in at least one state in our area. All are found in rocky or sandy areas with ample sun, such as grasslands, sagebrush flats, hillsides, and open woodlands, especially pinyon-juniper forests. They grow from the plains through the montane zones, and are common in semi-desert shrublands.

GROWTH: Prickly pear are composed of numerous flat, paddle-shaped succulent pads that branch off older segments; total height ranges from 4 inches to 10 feet. Pads have numerous *areoles*, rounded tuft-like buds spaced evenly along the skin. On most species, stiff spines grow from the areoles; the length and number of spines is one of the identifying characteristics among species. Areoles also have fine, barbed bristles called *glochids*. Flowers grow from fleshy green fruits that sit on top of the pads; flowers range from yellow to pink to orange to red, depending on species. Eventually, the flower falls off, and the fruit ripens to red or maroon.

LEAVES: No normal leaves; the spines may be considered modified leaves.

FRUIT: Shaped like a barrel or a flat-topped egg, prickly pear fruit (called *tuna*) grows from the top of the pad in rows or clusters. A cupped depression at the top shows where the flower was attached. Young fruits are green, maturing to red or maroon; they range from 1 to 3 inches long, depending on species and weather. All prickly pear fruits are edible; there are no toxic look-alikes. The flesh of ripe fruits is bright red, juicy and sweet, with many small, hard seeds; eating quality varies between species. *Caution: The fruits have fine, sharp bristles; handle with leather gloves, and singe over a flame before peeling.*

SEASON: Prickly pear flower from spring through midsummer; fruits are ripe from mid to late summer.

COMPARE: Nothing in the wild resembles a prickly pear.

NOTES: Prickly pear pads are also edible and delicious, and are called *nopales* when used in Mexican cooking. The glochids on prickly pear are found only on one other cactus family, the *Cylindropuntia* (pgs. 60, 120).

green = key identification feature   *combined range

Engelmann prickly pear
Opuntia engelmannii

Red flower

CACTUS

FALL

Pancake Pincushion Cactus *Mammillaria heyderi*

HABITAT: This native cactus is found in dry, sunny areas, including rocky hillsides and flats, grasslands and scrubby plateaus. It grows from the plains through the foothills, and is found in semi-desert shrublands.

GROWTH: A very low-growing, disk-shaped cactus, usually **an inch or less above the ground** during the summer. It is 3 to 6 inches across and grows as a solitary specimen. The surface is covered with rounded, pillowy bumps called *tubercles*; each is crowned with an *areole*, a rounded, tuft-like bud. Each areole has a single, dark ¼-inch-long upright spine, surrounded by a disk-like array of 10 to 26 straight, thin spines up to ¾ inch long that lie flat. In winter, the cactus sinks into the ground, rising back above ground level the following spring. *Mammillaria* stems contain a milk-like juice and are often referred to as nipple cactus for this reason. Salmon-colored blossoms grow between the tubercles in spring; they are eventually replaced by pod-like fruits.

LEAVES: No normal leaves; the spines may be considered modified leaves.

FRUIT: Elongated pod-like berries, about 1¼ inches long with smooth skins, grow upright between the tubercles; a brown floral remnant usually remains attached to the end. Fruits are green at first, ripening to **brilliant scarlet**. The ripe fruits, sometimes called "chilitos" because they **resemble red chile peppers**, have fleshy walls and a cavity in the center that is filled with brown seeds. The fruits are edible and generally sweet.

SEASON: Fruits ripen 6 months to a year after replacing the flowers, and are sometimes present during flowering the following spring.

COMPARE: MacDougal pincushion (*M. heyderi* ssp. *macdougalii*; see below for additional information) is related and very similar, but it is up to 3 inches high and its flowers are yellow rather than salmon-colored.

NOTES: There are five recognized subspecies of *M. heyderi*. Some sources consider these separate species; for example, the MacDougal pincushion noted above may be listed as *M. heyderi* ssp. *macdougalii* or as *M. macdougalii*, depending on the reference.

green = key identification feature

CACTUS

LATE SUMMER
THROUGH FALL

Desert Christmas Cactus

Cylindropuntia leptocaulis

HABITAT: This native shrub-like cactus is found in dry, sandy areas, including washes, overgrazed rangeland, grasslands, flats, mesa tops and scrubby areas from the plains through the foothills zones; it is common in semi-desert shrublands.

GROWTH: Christmas cactus looks like an open, much-branched shrub with long, sharp thorns; it often grows in wide, low prickly mounds or may be hidden among other shrubs. Stems are composed of pencil-like woody joints about ⅛ inch thick, which grow from a main trunk that often has tan scaly bark; total height is generally 1 to 3 feet, although they can grow taller when supported by adjacent trees or shrubs. Joints are grayish-green, sometimes streaked with purple. They have numerous *areoles*, rounded, tuft-like buds that typically have a single spine up to 2 inches long and several fine, barbed bristles called *glochids*. Yellow flowers grow along the stems from spring through summer; the plants may flower again in fall.

LEAVES: No normal leaves; the spines may be considered modified leaves.

FRUIT: Grape-shaped fruits about ½ inch long grow along the stems, often in profusion. The fruits are yellowish-green when immature, ripening to bright red. Each fruit has several whitish areoles with fine bristles. Ripe fruits are edible and sweet, and are often used to make jam. ***Caution: handle the fruits with leather gloves, and singe over a flame to remove the fine bristles before eating.***

SEASON: Fruits ripen from late summer through fall, and remain on the plants through winter; their colorful presence in December gives the plant its common name.

COMPARE: Other *Cylindropuntia* species grow in our area, but joints of the others are thicker and more fleshy. The pencil-like joints of Christmas cactus give it another of its common names, pencil cholla.

NOTES: Birds eat the fruits and often nest in the plants, whose thorns provide some protection from predators.

green = key identification feature

VINING
SUBSHRUB

ALTERNATE
LEAVES

LATE
SUMMER

Alpine Spicy Wintergreen

Gaultheria humifusa

HABITAT: This native plant requires cool, moist habitat and is typically found in conifer forests, on rocky forested slopes and along streambanks. It is most common in the sub-alpine to alpine zones, but may extend down to cool areas in the high foothills through the montane zone. At high altitudes, it may be found in damp meadows.

GROWTH: A ground-hugging, trailing plant, wintergreen is technically a sub-shrub, but vine-like in growth habit. It may grow as a small cluster or as a larger, mat-like colony. Individual stems may be up to 8 inches long, but the plant rarely rises higher than 2 inches from the ground. Stems have reddish hairs. All parts of the plant have a minty smell when crushed.

LEAVES: Leathery, shiny, hairless evergreen leaves grow alternately on short petioles (stemlets). Leaves are oval, broadest at or above the mid-point, with a rounded or slightly tapered base and a softly pointed tip; they are less than 1 inch in length and two-thirds as wide. Edges have very fine, bristle-tipped teeth (visible with a lens).

FRUIT: A smooth, squat, rounded red berry about ¼ inch wide and slightly less long; it has a star-shaped depression on the base. The berry is edible but mealy, with a mild wintergreen taste; it makes a decent trail nibble, but may cause problems if eaten in quantity. There are no toxic look-alikes.

SEASON: Fruits ripen in late summer.

COMPARE: Several similar-looking ground-hugging plants with edible fruits are found in our area. Western teaberry (*G. ovatifolia*) has red fruits, but its leaves are up to 1½ inches long; in our area, it is found only in northern Idaho and, rarely, in northwestern Montana. Bearberry (pg. 130) has red fruits and small leaves, but it lacks the minty smell. Creeping snowberry (*G. hispidula*) has a minty smell, but its fruit is white and its leaves are smaller, and the fruits, leaf undersides and stems have very fine, dark hairs; in our area, it is found only in two counties in northern Idaho.

NOTES: Leaves are often steeped to make tea. People who are sensitive to aspirin should not consume wintergreen due to possible allergic reaction.

green = key identification feature

WOODY
VINE

ALTERNATE
LEAVES

SUMMER
THROUGH FALL

Climbing Nightshade

Solanum dulcamara

HABITAT: Moist forests and thickets, swampy areas, waste ground, road-sides and streambanks. Climbing nightshade prefers partial shade and abundant moisture. It grows from the plains through the foothills.

GROWTH: A sprawling, non-native vine that produces many slim, scraggly branches that climb over other plants. It can appear as a short plant, but often grows to 10 feet in length, occasionally even longer. Branches are green or purplish and often hairy when young, turning brownish-green, smooth and woody as they mature; the base of the plant is woody. Flowers are bright purple with yellow centers. All parts of the plant have an unpleasant scent when crushed.

LEAVES: Bright green, shiny, heart-shaped leaves grow alternately on the branches; many leaves have two ear-like lobes at the base. The petioles (stemlets) are slightly flattened. Overall leaf length is up to 3 inches; the ear-like lobes span a width of up to 2 inches.

FRUIT: The glossy, many-seeded berry is up to ½ inch long and usually slightly narrower, although it can also be round rather than egg-shaped. Berries are green when immature, turning orange and finally bright red when ripe. All parts of the plant, including the berries, are highly toxic.

SEASON: Berries are produced throughout summer and into fall, remaining on the plant even after the leaves have fallen off.

COMPARE: Eastern black nightshade (pg. 250) has similar fruits, but it has tiny white flowers and its berries are black when ripe; leaves lack the lobes at the base, and the plant is a tender perennial that is only 1 to 3 feet in height.

NOTES: This plant is also called woody nightshade or bittersweet nightshade, a reference to the bittersweet compound dulcamarine, which is found in all parts of the plant, but especially the roots. It also contains solanine, a toxic alkaloid also found in the green parts of the common Irish potato (*S. tuberosum*) and other members of the nightshade family.

green = key identification feature

TENDER
VINE

ALTERNATE
LEAVES

LATE
SUMMER

Cutleaf Globeberry

Ibervillea tenuisecta

HABITAT: This native plant grows in well-drained sandy or rocky areas such as gullies, draws, washes, dry woods and rocky hillsides. It is a low-elevation species, found in the plains zone and in semi-desert shrublands.

GROWTH: A tender, perennial vine with a disk-like tuber called a caudex that may be up to a foot across; in the wild, the caudex is generally underground. The wiry stems are bluish-green and up to 9 feet long, with tendrils that they use to climb over shrubs or fences; the plants also crawl along the ground or over rocks. Globeberry plants are unisexual; a plant is either male or female, and each produces a different kind of flower and fruit.

LEAVES: Palmately lobed leaves up to 2½ inches across grow alternately from thick petioles (stemlets). The leaves are deep yellowish-green to bluish-green; top surfaces are smooth and dull, while the undersides are hairy. Most leaves have five narrow lobes with deep sinuses (the curved depressions between the lobes) that meet together in the center of the leaf; some leaves are three-lobed. Individual lobes have additional rounded lobes (like a tomato leaf); the overall effect is somewhat lacy.

FRUIT: Smooth, round berries, ½ to ¾ inch across, grow on short stemlets on female plants. Immature fruits are green with blotchy whitish stripes, resembling a tiny watermelon; ripe fruits are shiny, rich crimson red and resemble marbles. The fruits are not edible.

SEASON: Cutleaf globeberry produces tiny yellow flowers in early to mid summer; fruits are ripe in late summer.

COMPARE: Lindheimer's globeberry (*I. lindheimeri*) is a related vining plant, but its leaf lobes are much wider and its fruits are up to 1½ inches across. It grows in the wild primarily in southern Texas; in our area, it is found only in extreme southeastern New Mexico.

NOTES: Cutleaf globeberry often intertwines with thorny shrubs such as mesquite; these host plants protect the globeberry as it grows.

green = key identification feature

WOODY
VINE

OPPOSITE
LEAVES

LATE SUMMER
TO EARLY FALL

Orange

Arizona

Orange Honeysuckle –AND–
Arizona Honeysuckle

Lonicera spp.

HABITAT: Two native honeysuckle vines with red berries grow in our area: orange honeysuckle (*Lonicera ciliosa*) and Arizona honeysuckle (*L. arizonica*). They grow in the plains and montane zones, where they are found in open forests and thickets, clearings, and along streams and ravines.

GROWTH: A climbing woody vine, up to 20 feet in length; it may bend down upon itself and appear shrublike. Stems are smooth and hollow; trunks have shreddy bark. Long, trumpet-shaped flowers grow in a cluster at the end of the vine; orange honeysuckle has orange flowers, while those of Arizona honeysuckle are red or orangish-red.

LEAVES: Opposite, with a fringe of fine white hairs on the edges. The last pair of leaves at the end of the stem are joined at the bases to form a cup; leaf tips on this joined pair are typically pointed. Orange honeysuckle leaves are egg-shaped, 1½ to 4 inches long and one-half as wide; leaf surfaces are smooth and hairless with a white bloom underneath, and the petiole (stemlet) is quite short. Arizona honeysuckle leaves are oval, up to 2¾ inches long and two-thirds as wide; leaf surfaces are finely hairy and the petiole is about ⅓ inch long with sparse hairs.

FRUIT: Smooth, oval berries, about ⅜ inch long, grow on a stalk in a cluster from the center of the terminal leaf cup; berries have a bump on the bottom, and are reddish when ripe. They are very bitter; most references list them as inedible and possibly toxic, although some sources say they are edible but may cause vomiting. It's best to consider them inedible.

SEASON: Flowers are present from late spring through midsummer. The berries ripen from late summer through early fall.

COMPARE: Western white honeysuckle (*L. albiflora*) is a similar native vine with red berries, but its flowers are white; in our area it appears only in southwestern New Mexico.

NOTES: These honeysuckles are pollinated by hummingbirds.

green = key identification feature

Orange honeysuckle
fruits

Arizona honeysuckle
plant and flowers

VINING
SUBSHRUB

ALTERNATE
LEAVES

LATE SUMMER
THROUGH FALL

Bearberry –OR– Kinnikinnick

Arctostaphylos uva-ursi

HABITAT: Found in sandy or rocky areas in cool, open woodlands; forest and trail edges that are sunny and well drained; elevated shorelines. It grows from the plains through the montane zones.

GROWTH: A ground-hugging, trailing native plant, bearberry is technically a subshrub, but vine-like in growth habit. Often seen in a large, mat-like colony. Older stems can reach 3 feet in length; individual shoots rise up to 6 inches tall. Stems are flexible and reddish-brown; the thin bark is often shreddy on older stems.

LEAVES: Leathery, shiny, hairless evergreen leaves grow alternately on short petioles (stemlets) or clustered at branch tips; top sides are dark green and the undersides are pale green. Leaves are oval or paddle-shaped, broadest toward the tip, ⅜ to 1 inch in length and one-half as wide; edges are smooth and there is a noticeable fold at the midrib.

FRUIT: A glossy, round berry, about ⅓ inch in diameter, with a dimple at the bottom. Fruit is bright red when ripe. Bearberry is edible, but is mealy and not particularly flavorful. There are no toxic look-alikes.

SEASON: Fruits appear in late summer, ripening throughout late summer and fall. They may persist over winter if not eaten by wildlife.

COMPARE: Alpine spicy wintergreen (pg. 122) has similar red fruits, but its leaves have fine teeth on the edges; all parts of the plant smell spicy when crushed. Small cranberry (*Vaccinium oxycoccos*) has smaller, lance-shaped leaves that are white underneath; in our area it is only found in a few counties in upper Idaho.

NOTES: Bearberry leaves have been used medicinally, by American Indian peoples as well as physicians in Europe, to treat conditions including problems with the bladder, kidneys and urinary tract. The berries are a winter food source for bears and grouse.

green = key identification feature

PARASITIC SUBSHRUB

OPPOSITE LEAVES

LATE FALL

Juniper Mistletoe

Phoradendron juniperinum

HABITAT: This native plant is a parasitic subshrub that attaches itself to juniper trees (pg. 244); it has no intrinsic habitat of its own. It grows in semi-desert shrublands through the foothills zone.

GROWTH: A small, branching evergreen shrub that grows on juniper branches, juniper mistletoe is spread by birds, which deposit the seeds on tree branches either by wiping their beaks to remove the sticky pulp containing the seeds, or through droppings containing undigested seeds. The seeds adhere to the branches and develop roots, which parasitize the host tree. Mistletoe has fleshy stems, and grows in large, rounded clumps up to 3 feet across; it does not develop into a woody shrub-like plant. Stems are yellowish-green when young, turning orangish as they mature. It is typically noticed as a cluster of yellowish-green or orangish stems, which contrasts with the blue-green of the juniper foliage.

LEAVES: Tiny, scale-like leaves grow oppositely at the joints of the stems; they are so small that they are almost unnoticeable.

FRUIT: Translucent, glossy pinkish berries, about $\frac{3}{16}$ inch across, grow singly or in small clusters along the branches. The berries are juicy, with a single, bulb-shaped seed and extremely sticky pulp. Berries and all other parts of the plant are toxic to humans.

SEASON: Mistletoe berries ripen in late fall, and remain on the plants through late winter unless eaten by birds.

COMPARE: Oak mistletoe (*P. leucarpum*) is a very similar plant that parasitizes oak, Osage orange and other hardwoods, but its ripe berries are white; in our area, it is found only in southern New Mexico. Five species of dwarf mistletoe (*Arceuthobium* spp.) grow in our area; these parasitic subshrubs live on pine, fir and spruce and cause heavy damage. The overall plant is similar in appearance to juniper mistletoe, but the fruits are greenish or bluish and so small that they are typically not noticed.

NOTES: Juniper mistletoe primarily steals water from the host tree, unlike the more aggressive dwarf mistletoe, which also steals nutrients.

green = key identification feature

Ripe berries

SMALL
WOODY SHRUB

ALTERNATE
LEAVES

SUMMER

Thimbleberry

Rubus parviflorus

HABITAT: Openings in mixed-wood forests, along rural roads, edges and clearings. Produces more fruit in sunny areas with good moisture, but will tolerate some shade and somewhat dry soil. It grows from the plains through the montane zones.

GROWTH: An erect, open native shrub, 2 to 3 feet tall with equal spread, which often grows in large, open colonies. Older stems are reddish or gray, with shreddy bark; young stems are hairy. There are no thorns or prickles anywhere on the plant.

LEAVES: Large, light green leaves that resemble wrinkled maple leaves; 4 to 8 inches long and wide. Leaves have three to five pointed lobes, with coarsely toothy edges all around; they grow alternately on long petioles (stemlets). Undersides are paler and may be slightly hairy.

FRUIT: A compound drupe, ½ to ¾ inch across and fairly flat. Fruits are white and hard at first, turning pinkish and finally ripening to rich red; ripe fruits are very soft and juicy. Ripe fruits detach cleanly from the plant, leaving the receptacle (core) behind; the picked fruit is hollow, but so soft that it may crumble upon picking. Most foragers feel that ripe fruits are delicious, with a slight acidic tang that balances the sweetness; however, some foragers don't care for them at all, finding them too seedy and soft.

SEASON: Fruits develop in early summer, ripening in midsummer; typically, thimbleberries are beginning to ripen at the height of the red raspberry season, and continue to ripen after the raspberries are finished.

COMPARE: Boulder raspberries (pg. 136) have similar-appearing fruits, but the plant is larger with peeling, woody stems and its leaves are smaller. Red raspberries (pg. 138) also have similar fruits, but they grow as a prickly bramble with compound leaves and the fruits are more rounded. Please also see the text on pgs. 138 and 140 for information on other plants with similar fruits.

NOTES: Here's one plant that will never be commercialized; the ripe fruit is so soft that it falls apart easily, making it hard to pick and transport.

green = key identification feature

SMALL
WOODY SHRUB

ALTERNATE
LEAVES

MID TO
LATE SUMMER

Boulder Raspberry

Rubus deliciosus

HABITAT: This native shrub is found in rocky, well-drained areas with ample sun, including streambanks, ravines and slopes, from the plains through the foothills zones.

GROWTH: A woody, branching shrub that is typically 3 to 5 feet tall but can reach 9 feet in good conditions. Twigs are reddish-brown to tan and finely hairy; older stems are reddish with thin tan bark that splits vertically and flakes away in strips with curled edges. Boulder raspberry has no thorns or bristles.

LEAVES: The rounded leaves are smooth and medium green on top, with coarse teeth all around; undersides are paler and downy. They grow alternately on long petioles (stemlets) that are hairy and reddish-tan. Leaves are 1¼ to 2½ inches long and about equally wide, with five shallow lobes; the base is heart-shaped.

FRUIT: A compound drupe, about ½ inch across and fairly flat. Fruits are greenish and hard at first, turning pinkish and finally ripening to dark red or reddish-purple. The fruits are dry and seedy, with a fairly bland but not unpleasant flavor; they are not usually gathered by foragers. There are no toxic look-alikes in our area.

SEASON: White flowers, 1½ to 2¼ inches across, grow singly on long stemlets from leaf axils in early summer. Fruits replace the flowers, ripening in mid to late summer.

COMPARE: Thimbleberries (pg. 134) have similar flat compound drupes, but their leaves are larger with sharper, more defined lobes. Red raspberries (pg. 138) also have similar fruits, but they grow as a prickly bramble with compound leaves, and fruits are more rounded. Please also see the text on pgs. 138 and 140 for information on other plants with similar fruits.

NOTES: Boulder raspberry is one of the few members of the *Rubus* family (which includes raspberries and blackberries) that has simple leaves; most others have compound leaves. Some references list this plant as *Oreobatus deliciosus*.

green = key identification feature

DELICIOUS

SMALL
WOODY SHRUB

ALTERNATE
COMPOUND
LEAVES

SUMMER

Red Raspberry

Rubus idaeus

HABITAT: These native shrubs grow in open woods and thickets, and along edges; they are one of the first plants to appear in an area that has been cleared or burned. Grows from the foothills through the sub-alpine zones.

GROWTH: Red raspberries are brambles, sprawling vine-like shrubs that often form a thicket. Stems, called canes, grow to 5 feet in length, and are usually arching but may also be upright. Canes are prickly but have no thorns. Young canes are reddish or greenish in color; older canes are brownish and shreddy.

LEAVES: Compound, doubly-toothed leaves with sharply pointed tips grow alternately on the canes; undersides are pale. Leaves usually have three to five leaflets, occasionally seven; they are up to 8 inches long. The terminal leaflet has a short petiole (stemlet), while the side leaflets are attached directly to the stem.

FRUIT: A compound drupe with a rounded top, up to ½ inch across. Fruits are green and hard at first, ripening to rich red. Ripe fruits detach cleanly from the plant, leaving the receptacle (core) behind; the picked fruit is hollow. They are delicious, with no toxic look-alikes in our area.

SEASON: Red raspberries ripen in midsummer, generally after black raspberries and well before blackberries.

COMPARE: Thimbleberries (pg. 134) have large maple-like leaves, and the fruit is wider. Boulder raspberries (pg. 136) have peeling, woody stems and non-compound leaves. Dewberries (pg. 140) are low-growing plants with three-part compound leaves and smooth stems; the fruit does not detach easily from the receptacle. Underripe whitebark raspberries (pg. 254) resemble red raspberries, but the canes have large, heavy thorns and whitish stems. Blackberries (pgs. 252, 286) have similar fruits that are black when ripe; when red, they are hard and dry because they are underripe. Please also see the text on pg. 140 for additional look-alikes.

NOTES: One of the easiest wild berries to pick; it's easy to identify, widespread, plentiful and delicious. Some texts list this as *R. strigosus*.

green = key identification feature

SMALL
VINE-LIKE
SHRUB

ALTERNATE
COMPOUND
LEAVES

MID TO
LATE SUMMER

Dwarf Red Raspberry
–OR– **Dewberry**

Rubus pubescens

HABITAT: This native species prefers rich, moist areas, and is found in mixed or coniferous forests, swampy areas, damp thickets and low areas from the foothills through the montane zones.

GROWTH: A ground-hugging plant with long runners that creep along the ground, making it look more like a vine than a shrub. The plants spread by rooting at various points along the runners; leaves and flowers develop at these root nodes. Stems are smooth or slightly hairy, with no thorns or bristles. White flowers grow singly from leaf axils in early to midsummer.

LEAVES: Coarsely toothed three-part leaves with sharply pointed tips grow alternately on the trailing stem. Leaflets are smooth to somewhat hairy, and up to 2¼ inches long; total leaf length is 2½ to 4 inches.

FRUIT: The compound drupe, ¼ to ½ inch across, resembles a red raspberry; however, the ripe fruit of the dewberry does not separate easily from the receptacle (core). Ripe dewberries are edible and sweet, although quality and taste vary from one plant to another.

SEASON: Dewberries in our area ripen in mid to late summer.

COMPARE: Several other members of the *Rubus* family are low-growing. Nagoonberry (*R. arcticus*; also called dwarf raspberry) has pink flowers, and leaves that are much smaller and have blunt tips; in our area, it grows in only a few scattered counties in Montana, Wyoming and Colorado. Strawberry bramble (*R. pedatus*) has five-part leaves with blunt tips, and its compound fruit has larger individual drupelets; in our area, it grows only in northern Idaho and northwestern Montana. Fruits of trailing blackberry (pg. 252) are black when ripe. Please also see the text on pg. 138 for information on additional plants with fruits similar to dwarf red raspberry.

NOTES: If you find red dewberries that are hard and dry, they may be unripe trailing blackberries (pg. 252), which ripen to black. Let them ripen until soft, regardless of color, before harvesting.

green = key identification feature

SMALL
WOODY SHRUB

ALTERNATE
LEAVES

MID TO
LATE SUMMER

Garden Red Currant

Ribes rubrum

HABITAT: This European native is grown commercially, primarily in eastern Washington, and has escaped into the wild in scattered parts of our area. It inhabits cool, moist woodlands, swampy areas, clearings and streambanks; it may also be found on old homestead sites. Elevation information is not available for this plant, but it most likely would be found from the plains through the foothills zones.

GROWTH: An open, upright shrub that reaches 5 feet tall when cultivated but is usually shorter when found in the wild. Stems are smooth; older branches are woody and thornless.

LEAVES: Attached alternately to the stem by a medium to long petiole (stemlet). Each leaf has three to five distinct lobes with coarse, rounded teeth, somewhat resembling a maple leaf. Leaves are 1 to 2½ inches long and almost as wide; both surfaces are smooth.

FRUIT: Round ¼- to ⅜-inch berries grow in racemes (long clusters of multiple fruits). Immature berries are green, turning red and somewhat translucent when ripe. Berries are smooth and glossy; they are edible, and are tart but delicious when used in baking, or cooked into jelly, jam and other dishes. There are no toxic look-alikes.

SEASON: Garden red currants ripen in mid to late summer.

COMPARE: Swamp red currant (*R. triste*) is a native shrub that is similar in appearance, but it is a shorter plant that usually sprawls along the ground and its leaves are hairy underneath; in our area, it is found only occasionally in western Montana. Wax currants (pg. 166) have similar fruits and leaves, but both fruits and leaves are dotted with sticky glands. Gooseberries (pgs. 44, 172, 264, 266, 268) have similar leaves and growth habits, but all gooseberries have thorns at the leaf nodes; gooseberry fruits grow in clusters of two or three, in contrast to currant fruits, which grow in a raceme.

NOTES: If you find a currant with red berries, but they are hard and opaque, you may have found unripe black currants (pgs. 256, 262, 278, 280).

green = key identification feature

SMALL
WOODY SHRUB

ALTERNATE
LEAVES

LATE SUMMER
TO EARLY FALL

Grouse Whortleberry

Vaccinium scoparium

HABITAT: This native shrub is found in open, rocky woods with moist, acidic soil; it frequently grows under lodgepole pine and other conifers. It is most common in the sub-alpine zone, but also grows in the montane zone and on north-facing slopes in the foothills.

GROWTH: Grouse whortleberry is often described as "broom-like" due to its long, wiry green stems which are leafless on the lower part. It generally stands less than a foot tall; although individual stems may be as long as 20 inches, they often straggle sideways, making the plant appear shorter. The stems bend slightly at leaf axils and have squared edges.

LEAVES: Thin, light green oval leaves, generally ¼ to ½ inch long and one-half to one-third as wide, grow alternately, attached directly to the stems (sessile). Edges have fine teeth; leaves taper to a point on both ends.

FRUIT: Rounded berries, about ¼ inch across, grow singly on short stemlets near the upper ends of the stems; spacing is the same as the leaves, but often no leaf is present at the stemlet base. Ripe berries are red or reddish-purple with a slight dusty bloom; the base of the berry is slightly flattened and has a circular depression. Ripe berries are sweet and delicious, and can be eaten raw or cooked; they are so small that they are typically eaten in the field because it is difficult to gather a large enough quantity for cooking or jam-making. There are no toxic look-alikes.

SEASON: Berries are ripe from late summer to early fall.

COMPARE: Dwarf bilberry (pg. 230) is a related member of the *Vaccinium* group. It is about the same height and has similarly shaped leaves and fruit, but its leaves are twice as large and its stems are not bare near the base of the plant; its ripe fruit is larger and dusty blue.

NOTES: This plant is called grouse whortleberry (or grouse huckleberry) because several species of grouse are particularly fond of the berries. It is also called littleleaf huckleberry or red huckleberry, although the latter name is more commonly used to refer to *V. parvifolium*, a plant that grows along the West coast, from Alaska to California, but not in our area.

green = key identification feature

SMALL
WOODY SHRUB

ALTERNATE
COMPOUND
LEAVES

LATE SUMMER
TO EARLY FALL

*see below

Rose Hips (several)

Rosa spp.

HABITAT: Nine native rose varieties and seven introduced varieties are found in the wild in our area. They grow in clearings, thickets and open forests; on waste ground; and along lakes, streams and rivers. Roses grow from the plains through sub-alpine zones.

GROWTH: A bushy, multi-stemmed shrub, typically 1 to 4 feet in height, with equal spread, roses sometimes grow as a bramble (a vine-like shrub with arching branches). Stems are armed with **thorns or prickles**, which may be scattered or may blanket the stem thickly. Bark of larger stems is shiny and typically reddish-brown; smaller stems are green.

LEAVES: Compound leaves, each with three to eleven oval leaflets, grow alternately. Leaflets are bright green above and typically have fine hairs on the underside; edges are sharply toothed. The compound leaf is typically between 2 to 4 inches long, usually slightly less wide.

FRUIT: The fruits, called hips, develop at the base of the flower; specific characteristics are quite variable. They range in shape from round to oval; ripe hips are red or orangish. Hips always have a group of **withered sepals at the end of the fleshy swelling**. All hips are edible, but they are filled with small, bitter seeds and tiny, stiff, irritating hairs. The best hips for eating have a higher flesh-to-seed ratio. There are no toxic look-alikes.

SEASON: Roses bloom from late spring through summer; hips develop afterwards and are hard and green most of the summer, ripening in late summer to early fall. They typically persist through winter, and become softer and sweeter after a frost.

COMPARE: Roses are easy to identify, especially when hips (or flowers) are present; no other plant compares to a rose.

NOTES: Rose hips are rich in nutrients, particularly vitamin C. They may be eaten raw or cooked; split the hips and scrape out the bitter seeds and irritating hairs before eating. Palatability varies between species and also from plant to plant, so try a few from the plants you've found before collecting too many. Rose hips are often dried and brewed for tea.

green = key identification feature

*combined range

SMALL
WOODY SHRUB

ALTERNATE
LEAVES

MID TO
LATE SUMMER

Javelina Bush

Condalia ericoides

HABITAT: This small native shrub is found in areas of desert scrub; it grows in the plains, foothills and semi-desert shrubland zones.

GROWTH: This thorny, multi-branched shrub appears very open because its leaves are so tiny. It is **2 to 4½ feet high** with equal spread; branches tend to grow at an outward angle from the base rather than upright. Twigs and stems are gray; older stems are very rough-textured. Stems are tipped with short but sharp spines; additional spines grow along the stems. From late spring through summer, the plant is covered with tiny yellow blooms shaped like five-pointed stars.

LEAVES: Narrow, strap-shaped leaves grow in small clusters that alternate along the stem; they do not have a petiole (stemlet). Leaves are ⅛ to ½ inch long and about ¹⁄₁₆ inch wide; they are light green, and the edges are curled under.

FRUIT: Football-shaped drupes about ¾ inch long grow on short stemlets. Fruits have a small cap on top and a very short tail on the bottom; they are brick-red, bright red or purplish-black when ripe. Although fruits of related *Condalia*, such as Warnock's snakewood (pg. 284), are known to be edible, information about the edibility of javelina bush fruits is not available; it's best to consider them inedible.

SEASON: Fruits ripen from mid to late summer.

COMPARE: Warnock's snakewood (pg. 284) is a similar-looking thorny plant, but it is up to 10 feet tall; its leaves are paddle-shaped and its ripe fruits are black drupes. Lotebush (pg. 242) is also similar, but it is a taller shrub and its ripe fruits are dusty-looking dark blue berries.

NOTES: The dense, thorny branches of javelina bush provide nesting protection for birds. Some references list this plant as *Microrhamnus ericoides*.

green = key identification feature

SMALL
WOODY SHRUB

OPPOSITE
LEAVES

FALL

Coralberry –OR– Buckbrush *Symphoricarpos orbiculatus*

HABITAT: This native shrub is found only occasionally in our area in dry, sunny locations, including pastures, roadsides, rocky bluffs, thickets and open woods. It grows in the plains and foothills zones.

GROWTH: An open, twiggy, multi-stemmed shrub, up to 4 feet in height but often shorter; it spreads by rhizomes (underground root-bearing stems) and often forms large colonies. Branches are thin and flexible, often arching downward, especially when bearing fruit. Young stems are tan to purplish and downy, later becoming smooth and brown. The trunk has flaky or shreddy brown bark.

LEAVES: Egg-shaped, with a rounded or tapered base and roundly pointed tip; 1½ to 2 inches long and two-thirds as wide, broadest at or below the midpoint. Leaves grow oppositely on very short petioles (stemlets); the edges are untoothed, and may have fine hairs (visible with a lens). The top surface is bluish-green and smooth; undersides are paler and typically hairy, with pronounced veins.

FRUIT: Tight, sometimes blocky clusters of round to egg-shaped drupes, each about ¼ inch long, grow at leaf axils and at the tips of the branches; a crown-like floral remnant is present on the base. The fruits are opaque, rosy reddish-purple when ripe. They are not edible.

SEASON: Tiny, greenish flowers appear underneath the leaves at the leaf axils in midsummer; fruits develop slowly, ripening in fall. The fruits may persist over winter unless eaten by wildlife.

COMPARE: Bush honeysuckles (pg. 164) have numerous berries along the stem, but they are bright red or orange and translucent, and the shrubs are much larger than coralberry when mature.

NOTES: The leaves and twigs are browsed by deer and other mammals; birds sometimes nest in the dense growth, and some eat the fruits, although they do not appear to be a favored food. This plant is sometimes called Indian currant, a reference to the appearance of the fruits.

green = key identification feature

LARGE
WOODY SHRUB

ALTERNATE
LEAVES

SUMMER
THROUGH FALL

Matrimony Vine –OR– Goji Berry *Lycium barbarum*

HABITAT: Also called wolfberry, this Asian native is grown as an ornamental and has escaped into the wild, where it is found from the plains through the foothills. It prefers sun and requires well-drained soil; it grows on disturbed sites, alongside roads and fences, and in abandoned fields.

GROWTH: A somewhat sprawling, straggly shrub with thin branches; longer branches **droop down and scramble along the ground**. The stems are brownish, sometimes mottled with pale gray; thin lengthwise ridges are often present. Older bark is rough. Plants may have short thorns.

LEAVES: Lance-shaped, or sometimes oval with tapered ends; **tips are pointed**. Leaves are **up to 2½ inches long** and one-third to one-half as wide; the base tapers into a short, wide petiole (stemlet). Leaves grow alternately, sometimes in small clusters. Edges are smooth; the midrib is prominent. Both surfaces are smooth and dull green in color.

FRUIT: Oval berries, ¼ inch long and half as wide, grow on long stemlets from the leaf axils; the berry is joined to the stemlet with a **bell-shaped cap**. The berries are reddish-orange when ripe, and contain numerous small seeds. Fully ripe berries are sweet, and are edible raw or cooked. Underripe berries may contain toxins and should not be consumed.

SEASON: **Purple, bell-shaped flowers** bloom from late spring through early fall; berries ripen throughout summer and into fall.

COMPARE: Pale wolfberry (pg. 158) is related, but it its leaves are pale, smaller and paddle-shaped and its fruit has a frilly cap. Berlandier's wolfberry (*L. berlandieri*) is also related, but its fruits are round; in our area, it is found only in the southern half of New Mexico. Climbing nightshade (pg. 124) is a woody vine with similar berries, but its leaves are broader and heart-shaped; nightshade berries are toxic.

NOTES: Pioneers heading to Utah planted wolfberry around cemeteries to protect the graves; some of those plants are still growing today. Goji is grown commercially in China; dried berries are sold here and abroad for use in cooking. The juice is marketed in the U.S. as a health tonic.

green = key identification feature

Thorns

LARGE
WOODY SHRUB

OPPOSITE
COMPOUND
LEAVES

SUMMER

Red Elderberry

Sambucus racemosa var. *racemosa*

HABITAT: This native shrub is found in cool, moist areas, such as openings and edges of conifer and mixed-wood forests; it prefers sun but will tolerate some shade. It grows from the foothills through the sub-alpine zones.

GROWTH: A large, fast-growing native shrub. Up to 20 feet in height, but typically found much shorter. Bark of older stems is gray to reddish-brown, and covered with numerous warty lenticels (breathing pores). Younger stems are soft and pithy, and often covered with downy hairs.

LEAVES: Compound leaves, each with five to seven leaflets, grow oppositely on the stem; leaves are 6 to 10 inches long and nearly as wide. Leaflets are 2 to 5 inches long and one-third as wide, oval with a rounded base and pointed tip; edges have fine, sharp teeth. Top sides are dark green and smooth, undersides are paler and may be downy.

FRUIT: Round drupes, about ⅛ inch across, with two seeds, grow profusely in upright, rounded clusters atop stalks that rise from the leaf axils; fruits are bright red when ripe. The fruits are rank in flavor and somewhat toxic, especially when raw; cooking may render the fruit—but not the seeds—edible, but opinions vary. Leaves, stems and all other parts of all elderberry species are toxic.

SEASON: Red elderberry flowers in spring, while the leaves are still unfolding. Fruits ripen from early to late summer, depending on altitude and specific conditions.

COMPARE: Rocky Mountain elderberry (pg. 274) is very similar, but ripe fruits are black to purplish-black. Common elderberry (pg. 212) has similar growth habits, but ripe fruits are purplish-black and grow in flat-topped clusters rather than the rounded clusters of red elderberry; common elderberry leaves have five to 11 leaflets. Fruits of common elderberry are edible when cooked.

NOTES: The fruits are eaten by many species of birds and other wildlife. Some sources list this plant as *S. pubens*; others list it as *S. racemosa* var. *leucocarpa* or *S. microbotrys*.

green = key identification feature

LARGE
WOODY SHRUB

ALTERNATE
LEAVES

SUMMER

Wild Crabapple

Peraphyllum ramosissimum

HABITAT: This native shrub is found in sunny, well-drained areas, including open woodlands, scrublands, dry hills, low mesas, waste fields and middle-elevation slopes. It often grows alongside sagebrush in areas dominated by scrub oak, and in pinyon-juniper forests. It can tolerate dry, hot conditions and is found from the foothills through the montane zone.

GROWTH: A stiff-branched, brushy-looking shrub, wild crabapple grows to 6 feet tall, with nearly equal spread. Multiple gray branches spread outward from the base in a dense growth pattern; the overall shape is vaselike. Wild crabapples often form scrubby, weedy-looking colonies.

LEAVES: Small, narrow, paddle- to lance-shaped leaves grow alternately, or in tight clusters along the branches and at branch tips. Leaves are smooth and bright green on both surfaces; they are generally less than an inch long. Edges may be smooth, or may have small teeth around the top half.

FRUIT: Rounded pomes, generally ⅜ to ½ inch across, grow singly or in small clusters on sturdy ½-inch stemlets. Each fruit has a prominent five-pointed crown on the bottom. Fruits are greenish when underripe, turning yellow with a reddish blush as they ripen; fully ripe fruits are a dusty red. Ripe fruits are edible, but they are somewhat bitter and contain hard seeds. There are no toxic look-alikes.

SEASON: Highly fragrant white flowers blanket the shrubs in late spring. Ripe fruits are generally present from late June through August.

COMPARE: This plant, which is also called by the racially offensive name of squaw apple, is in a different genus from all other crabapples (*Malus* spp.); most wild *Malus* grow in the midwestern, eastern and southeastern U.S. but not in our area. Serviceberries (pg. 216) are large shrubs or small trees that have similar fruits, but the fruits are rich red, purple or bluish-black when ripe; the leaves are oval-shaped and up to 3 inches long.

NOTES: Fruits can be used to make jelly, although it may be an acquired taste (H. D. Harrington; *Edible Native Plants of the Rocky Mountains*).

green = key identification feature

LARGE
WOODY SHRUB

ALTERNATE
LEAVES

SUMMER

Pale Wolfberry

Lycium pallidum

HABITAT: This native shrub inhabits hot, well-drained areas such as desert grasslands, openings in pinyon-juniper forests, dry canyons, rocky slopes and hillsides; it is found in washes and other areas where runoff provides occasional moisture. It inhabits the plains through the lower foothills zones and is common in semi-desert shrublands.

GROWTH: Multi-branched, dusty-looking shrubs, 3 to 5 feet tall; they often grow as a thicket. Branches range from reddish-brown to tan to gray; the bark is smooth but the branches are bumpy at leaf nodes. Older bark is rough-textured and may split lengthwise. Pale wolfberry has numerous thin, sharp thorns up to ⅓ inch long along the branches; if the plant is densely leafy as in the photo at right, the thorns may be hard to see.

LEAVES: Slightly thick, paddle-shaped leaves with a tapered base grow alternately or in small clusters; they are typically ½ to 1¾ inches long. The top surface is dull, pale greenish gray and the lower surface is slightly lighter in color; the midvein is prominent on both surfaces.

FRUIT: Egg-shaped berries with a broad top and a tapering, rounded bottom grow singly or in small groups on thin stemlets from leaf clusters. Ripe fruits are about ½ inch long, and reddish to reddish-orange with a whitish bloom. Berries have a frilly cap on top that is similar to the cap on a strawberry but not as leafy. Ripe fruits are sweet and edible in moderation.

SEASON: Pale wolfberry flowers throughout summer after rain; fruits follow and may be present all summer depending on weather.

COMPARE: Goji berry (pg. 152) is related, but its fruits are smaller and lack the frilly cap, and its leaves are longer and darker green.

NOTES: According to "Ethnobotany of the Zuñi Indians" in the *Annual Report of the Bureau of American Ethnology to the Secretary of the Smithsonian Institution*, Volume 30, Parts 1908–1909: "The berries [of *Lycium pallidum*] are boiled, and, if not entirely ripe, they are sometimes sweetened. This dish, which is regarded as a great delicacy, is called kĭa' puli mo'li, 'water-fall-down berry' . . . the berries are also eaten raw when fully ripe."

green = key identification feature

LARGE
WOODY SHRUB

OPPOSITE
LEAVES

MID TO
LATE SUMMER

Utah Honeysuckle

Lonicera utahensis

HABITAT: This native shrub, also called red twinberry, grows in moist areas, including stream valleys and bog edges; also found in canyons and on slopes. It grows in mixed-conifer forests containing ponderosa, white and lodgepole pines, and other conifers such as Douglas fir, cedar and spruce. It is found from the foothills to sub-alpine elevations.

GROWTH: Utah honeysuckle is a multi-branched upright shrub, typically 3 to 6 feet tall; it can be open and sparse or fairly full, and often grows in clumps. Stems are reddish-gray to brownish; the trunk is reddish-brown and dotted with pale lenticels (breathing pores). White to yellow tubular flowers grow in pairs from leaf axils on ½- to 1-inch stemlets.

LEAVES: Opposite, elliptic leaves with a short petiole (stemlet) are generally ¾ to 3 inches long and one-half to two-thirds as wide; tips are usually slightly rounded but may end in a short point. Edges are untoothed and have fine hairs; leaves are smooth above with scattered hairs below.

FRUIT: Paired oblong red berries are connected at the base and grow on a stalk originating in the leaf axil. Berries taper to a rounded point; each berry is ¼ to ⅜ inch long. The berries are fairly sweet but bland. Many sources list them as edible but not worth seeking out; some sources state that the fruits cause digestive problems for some individuals and should not be eaten. Utah honeysuckle are generally not prolific fruit producers; berries are noticeable due to their color, not their profusion.

SEASON: Flowers bloom from spring through early summer; fruits are ripe in mid to late summer.

COMPARE: Some bush honeysuckles (pg. 164) have similar form and leaves, but the berries are separate rather than paired, and are more numerous. Canada fly honeysuckle (*L. canadensis*) is a very similar plant with paired red berries, but it does not grow in the West.

NOTES: Grizzly and black bears, and upland birds such as ruffed grouse, eat the berries; elk and moose browse on the leaves and twigs.

green = key identification feature

LARGE
WOODY SHRUB

ALTERNATE
LEAVES

LATE
SUMMER

Greenleaf Manzanita

Arctostaphylos patula

HABITAT: This native shrub prefers sunny, well-drained rocky or sandy areas, and is found in open coniferous and mixed-wood forests, in canyons, and on disturbed sites, often in areas that have been swept by fire. It tolerates drought, and may be found tucked under conifers on rocky, sparsely vegetated mountaintops, in association with prickly pear cactus (pg. 116). It grows from the foothills through the montane zones, and is found in semi-desert shrublands.

GROWTH: A sturdy, many-branched shrub up to 7 feet tall but typically shorter; branches are usually twisted and crooked-looking. Greenleaf manzanita branches spread sideways, and individual plants may be up to 10 feet wide. Young stems are greenish and hairy. Branches have bark that is smooth and reddish to reddish-brown; it often splits and peels on larger branches, revealing the pale wood underneath.

LEAVES: Thick, leathery leaves grow alternately on moderately long petioles (stemlets); they grow horizontally or stand upright rather than hanging down. Leaves are oval to egg-shaped with softly pointed tips; they are up to 2 inches long and two-thirds to three-quarters as wide. Edges and both leaf surfaces are smooth; the midvein is prominent on both sides.

FRUIT: Tight clusters of rounded drupes grow on stemlets from branch tips; fruits are roughly ⅓ inch across with a thread-like style (floral remnant) on the base. The fruits are green when immature, gradually ripening to shiny red. The flesh is mealy, and there are several hard seeds. Fully ripe fruits are edible raw or cooked, with a tart flavor that resembles green apples; the seeds are hard and astringent.

SEASON: Greenleaf manzanita flowers in late spring to early summer; fruits are ripe in late summer.

COMPARE: Bearberry (pg. 130) is a related but much smaller plant; it sometimes hybridizes with greenleaf manzanita.

NOTES: The crooked branches, with their smooth, reddish bark, are used by crafters to make attractive lamp bases and other decorative pieces.

green = key identification feature

LARGE
WOODY SHRUB

OPPOSITE
LEAVES

EARLY SUMMER
THROUGH FALL

*see below

Bush Honeysuckles (several)

Lonicera spp.

HABITAT: Four types of non-native bush honeysuckles with red or orange-red berries inhabit our region. Tatarian honeysuckle (*Lonicera tatarica*) is the most common, and is found in all states in our area. Morrow's honeysuckle (*L. morrowii*) is in a few counties of all states in our area except Idaho; showy bush honeysuckle (*L. × bella*) is in a few counties each in Wyoming, Colorado and New Mexico, and winter honeysuckle (*L. fragrantissima*) is found only in a small part of Utah. All are considered invasive. They inhabit forest edges, parklands and shelterbelts. Highly adaptable, they prefer full sun with ample moisture, but tolerate shade and moderately dry soil. They are generally found in the plains zone.

GROWTH: Multi-stemmed shrubs with spreading crowns. Bark on older branches is often shreddy, peeling off in vertical strips. Tatarian and Morrow's honeysuckle are very similar, while showy bush honeysuckle is a hybrid between the two, with intermediate characteristics. Tatarian honeysuckle can grow to 14 feet tall; Morrow's is 13 feet or less. Showy bush and winter honeysuckles are 10 feet or less.

LEAVES: Opposite, oval, blue-green leaves, 1 to 2½ inches long, with short petioles (stemlets). Morrow's are hairy on both surfaces and have hairy edges; Tatarian's leaves are smooth on both surfaces with hairy edges, while those of showy bush honeysuckle are moderately to sparsely hairy. Winter honeysuckle's leaves are smooth and hairless.

FRUIT: A juicy, round berry, ¼ inch in size; most are red when ripe, but some are orange even when ripe. Berries often grow in pairs and may appear to be joined at the base, but each berry is distinctly round. Fruits of all non-native honeysuckles are bitter and inedible.

SEASON: Bush honeysuckles are one of the first plants to develop leaves in the spring. Ripe berries are present from early summer through fall.

COMPARE: Utah honeysuckle (pg. 160) does not exceed 6 feet; its red paired fruits are joined at the base and have pointed tips.

NOTES: Birds devour honeysuckle berries, propagating the plants.

green = key identification feature

*combined range

Orange berries

LARGE
WOODY SHRUB

ALTERNATE
LEAVES

MID TO
LATE SUMMER

Wax Currant

Ribes cereum

HABITAT: This native shrub thrives in warm, sunny areas with fairly dry or rocky soil; it is found in forest openings and canyons, on mountain slopes and sagebrush flats, and under ponderosa pines and sparse conifers. It grows from the foothills through the sub-alpine zones.

GROWTH: An upright, stiff-branched shrub up to 6 feet high but usually shorter. Young stems are moderately hairy and greenish or grayish, becoming smooth and reddish-brown; the oldest branches are gray and hairless, often with peeling bark. Wax currant has no prickles or thorns. The leaves and fruit have a pleasant, spicy fragrance.

LEAVES: Broad, fan-shaped leaves, up to 1⅝ inches across and usually slightly shorter, grow alternately on thick, hairy petioles (stemlets) that are roughly the same length as the leaves. Leaves have a heart-shaped base and coarse, rounded teeth on the edges above the base; some leaves appear rounded with no lobes, while others have three to five fairly shallow lobes. The upper surface is dark green; it has a waxy coating and numerous tiny, bump-like glands (visible with a lens). The lower surface is paler and covered with hairs and sticky glands.

FRUIT: Rounded berries about ⅓ inch across grow singly or in short, hanging clusters from leaf axils; a prominent flower remnant, often called a pigtail, is present at the end of the berry. Ripe berries are translucent, and dull to bright red; they have numerous small hair-like glands on the surface that secrete a sticky fluid. They are juicy and mildly sweet, but may cause digestive problems in some people. There are no toxic look-alikes.

SEASON: Fruits are ripe from mid to late summer.

COMPARE: Sticky currant (pg. 278) has similar leaves, but they are larger and more sticky, with deeper lobes; ripe fruit is black. Gooseberry currant (pg. 172) has red fruits and leaves with white hairs, but its leaves are larger and have much deeper lobes.

NOTES: The species name, *cereum*, means "waxy" and is a reference to the waxy coating on the leaves.

green = key identification feature

Glands on leaf

LARGE
WOODY SHRUB

ALTERNATE
COMPOUND
LEAVES

MID TO
LATE SUMMER

Three-Leaf Sumac

Rhus trilobata

HABITAT: Well-drained areas, including grasslands, pinyon-juniper forests, rocky slopes, hillsides, streambanks, shrubby areas and old pastures. It prefers sun, but will tolerate light shade. It grows from the plains through the montane zones and is found in semi-desert shrublands.

GROWTH: A spreading, multi-branched shrub, typically 4 to 6 feet tall and up to 6 feet wide; with ample moisture, it can grow to 12 feet tall. Twigs are tan and hairy when young; older stems are gray and smooth. Numerous branches usually rise above the mound of base foliage. When crushed, leaves and stems emit a strong scent that some find unpleasant, giving rise to an alternate common name of skunkbush.

LEAVES: Glossy three-part leaves with scalloped edges grow alternately on long, reddish petioles (stemlets). Leaves are 2 to 3 inches long, dark green on top and lighter below. The end leaflet is generally larger than the side leaflets and joined to them by a long, tapering neck.

FRUIT: Clusters of rounded, hairy, reddish-orange drupes, each about ¼ inch long, grow at branch tips. The drupes are lemony-sour, and can be used to make a lemonade-type beverage. There are no toxic look-alikes with hairy, red fruits; however, people who are highly allergic to poison ivy, mangoes or cashews should avoid all sumacs, which are in the same family and may cause a severe allergic reaction.

SEASON: Fruits ripen in mid to late summer and often persist into winter.

COMPARE: Poison ivy (pg. 304) has three-part leaves that may have scalloped edges, but it has small ribbed berries that are greenish or white; also, the end leaflet of poison ivy has a long stemlet. Fragrant sumac (*R. aromatica*) is very similar in appearance to three-leaf sumac, but its leaves are slightly larger and the plant is generally shorter; it is primarily an eastern plant, found only as far west as Kansas and Oklahoma.

NOTES: American Indian women often use the stems for basketry; some sources refer to this plant by the racially offensive name of squawbush. Some sources list this plant as *R. aromatica* var. *trilobata*.

green = key identification feature

LARGE
WOODY SHRUB

ALTERNATE
COMPOUND
LEAVES

MID TO
LATE SUMMER

Fremont's Mahonia –OR–
Desert Oregon Grape

Mahonia fremontii

HABITAT: This native shrub is found in well-drained rocky, sandy or gravelly areas, such as desert scrublands, plateaus and open woodlands, particularly pinyon-juniper forests. It tolerates drought but does poorly in areas that freeze; it grows primarily in semi-desert shrublands.

GROWTH: An open, sometimes straggly-looking shrub with stiff, thick branches, Fremont's mahonia grows to 10 feet tall. It has very few side branches; the compound leaves often grow directly from the main branches. Bark is reddish-brown, turning gray-brown and developing fissures, ridges and rough spots with age. The inner bark is yellow.

LEAVES: Compound leaves grow alternately, from scattered side branches or directly from the larger branches. Leaves are 4 to 5½ inches long; each has 3 to 9 leathery leaflets attached directly to the main leaf stem, which is thin and pale. Leaflets are typically 1 to 2 inches long and are holly-like, with an average of 5 to 7 sharply pointed, spine-tipped teeth. Young leaflets are yellowish-green, turning blue-green with a dusty whitish coating. The leaves remain on the shrubs through winter.

FRUIT: Rounded berries, ½ inch across and up to ¾ inch long, grow on long, thin stemlets. The berries may be rounded or lumpy; they often have a vertical cleft. Unripe berries are green and hard, turning yellow before ripening to dusty rose-red. Sources list them as edible although very sour; however, ripe berries are dry and sponge-like or hollow, offering little to eat. There are no toxic look-alikes that have compound leaves with holly-like leaflets.

SEASON: Yellow flowers are profuse in spring through early summer; fruits ripen in mid to late summer. The plants may bloom again in the fall.

COMPARE: Holly-leaved barberry (pg. 240) is a tall shrub with holly-like compound leaves, but it produces tight clusters of small bluish berries.

NOTES: Sharp leaves provide cover for small birds while they eat the berries.

green = key identification feature

LARGE
WOODY SHRUB

ALTERNATE
LEAVES

LATE
SUMMER

Gooseberry Currant

Ribes montigenum

HABITAT: This native shrub is found on dry, rocky sites, including high meadows, boulder fields and rocky ridges; it also grows in damp areas such as ravines, streambanks and moist woodlands. It grows from the montane through the alpine zones.

GROWTH: A woody shrub up to 5 feet tall; the branches often spread sideways or recline slightly, making the shrub appear shorter. Stems are buff- to cinnamon-colored and usually hairy or bristly, giving rise to another common name, alpine prickly currant. Older bark is brownish-gray to brownish-red, and often knobby in appearance. Leaf nodes have up to three sharp spines that are about ¼ inch long.

LEAVES: Alternate, up to 1½ inches long and slightly wider, growing singly or in small clusters on long petioles (stemlets) that are generally shorter than the leaves. Each leaf has three to five deeply divided lobes with rounded teeth; both surfaces are covered with white hairs that are somewhat sticky.

FRUIT: Round berries, ¼ to ⅓ inch across, grow from leaf axils in racemes (long clusters of multiple fruits; racemes of gooseberry currant are fairly short). The berries are translucent red when ripe, and are covered with short, dark hairs. A short flower remnant is present at the end of the berry. Although the hairs may look unappealing, they are quite soft, and the berries are sweet and juicy. There are no toxic look-alikes.

SEASON: Saucer-shaped pink to orangish flowers appear in early to mid-summer. Fruits follow, and are ripe in late summer.

COMPARE: Wax currant (pg. 166) has red fruits and leaves with white hairs, but its leaves are smaller and are shallowly lobed. Orange gooseberry (*R. pinetorum*) has spine-covered reddish berries; in our area, it grows only in southwestern New Mexico. Prickly currant (pg. 280) has bristly stems, but its leaves are smooth and up to 2 inches long; ripe fruits are black.

NOTES: Because this plant is found at high elevations, it is sometimes called mountain gooseberry. It often grows under Engelmann spruce.

green = key identification feature

LARGE
WOODY SHRUB

ALTERNATE
LEAVES

LATE
SUMMER

Devil's Club

Oplopanax horridus

HABITAT: This native shrub grows in moist, shady woods, and is often found near streams, waterfalls or spring seeps. It is an understory plant in old-growth forests, and is found in association with redcedar, western hemlock, huckleberries, blueberries and ferns. It grows from the plains through the foothills zones.

GROWTH: Devil's club is a very prickly shrub that often grows in colonies; it typically grows upright but may also recline or bend itself around rocks. It is 3 to 10 feet tall, and often has only one main stem. Bark is tan and densely covered with variously sized prickles; young stems are green. A conical cluster of small white flowers grows at the top of the stem.

LEAVES: Palmately lobed leaves, 5 to 15 inches across, grow alternately from the main stem on very long, prickly petioles (stemlets). Leaves have five to seven lobes with sharp tips and several large, sharp teeth; they resemble very large maple leaves. Top surfaces are bright green and the undersides are paler. The main veins are prominent, meeting at the heart-shaped base of the leaf; the veins have prickles on the underside.

FRUIT: A long, rounded cluster of small, shiny, bright red drupes grows at the top of the stem, replacing the flowers. The cluster typically grows upright, but it sometimes grows sideways. The fruits are inedible.

SEASON: Flowers appear in early to mid summer; fruits are ripe in late summer. The plants drop their leaves following a frost.

COMPARE: Red elderberry (pg. 154) has a cluster of small, bright red fruits at the top of the stem, but the similarities stop there.

NOTES: Devil's club populations are being reduced by habitat destruction; it is a slow-growing plant and takes years to form a colony. The root of devil's club is used medicinally to treat various conditions, including diabetes, infection, arthritis and skin conditions. The spines can cause severe skin irritation; take care not to wander into a colony of devil's club. Grizzly and black bear seem immune to the effects and frequently eat the berries, leaves and stems.

green = key identification feature

LARGE
WOODY SHRUB

OPPOSITE
LEAVES

LATE SUMMER
TO EARLY FALL

Squashberry

Highbush
cranberry

Squashberry –AND–
Highbush Cranberry

Viburnum spp.

HABITAT: These related native plants prefer cool, moist areas with moderate shade such as sun-dappled forests, thickets, swampy areas, river valleys, rocky streambanks and woodland edges. Both grow from the plains to the foothills; squashberry extends into the montane zone.

GROWTH: Multi-stemmed, leafy shrubs with rounded crowns. Twigs are reddish-gray; older stems are grayish-brown, often becoming rough with age. Squashberry (*Viburnum edule*) is generally 6 feet or shorter, but can grow taller in good conditions; highbush cranberry (*V. opulus* var. *americanum;* formerly named *V. trilobum*) can be up to 15 feet tall.

LEAVES: Three-lobed, maple-like leaves grow oppositely on ½- to 1-inch petioles (stemlets) that are grooved. Squashberry leaves are 2 to 4 inches long and wide, with numerous sharp teeth and fairly shallow lobes; leaves at the ends of branches may be unlobed. Highbush cranberry leaves are up to 5 inches long and slightly less wide; teeth are shallow and rounded, and lobes are deeper.

FRUIT: Shiny, bright red drupes, ¼ to ½ inch long with a single, large pit, grow in flat-topped clusters; squashberries are generally round, while highbush cranberry fruits tend to be oval. Highbush cranberry clusters grow on a long, reddish stalk that extends from the branch tip, beyond the last pair of leaves. Squashberry clusters grow on a stalk that extends from a very short side branch that has a single pair of leaves. Ripe, soft fruits of both are tart but edible, with a taste similar to cranberries; they are used to make jelly, jam or sauce. There are no toxic look-alikes.

SEASON: Fruits ripen in late summer to early fall, and may persist on the plant through winter. Leaves turn red or golden in fall.

COMPARE: Maple trees (*Acer* spp.) have similar leaves but lack the red fruits.

NOTES: Highbush cranberry clusters often have a dozen or more fruits; squashberry has a small number of fruits per cluster.

green = key identification feature

Squashberry

Highbush cranberry

LARGE
WOODY SHRUB

ALTERNATE
LEAVES

LATE SUMMER
TO EARLY FALL

Colorado

Common

Barberries (several)

Berberis spp.

HABITAT: Two barberry varieties are locally common in our area. The native Colorado barberry (*Berberis fendleri*) grows in openings in rich, mixed-wood forests (particularly scrub oak/ponderosa pine) and may also be found along streams and cliffs; it is most common from the foothills through the montane zones. Common barberry (*B. vulgaris*) is a non-native cultivated plant that has naturalized in the wild, where it is found in woodlands, abandoned fields and along roadsides in the plains zone.

GROWTH: Both are upright shrubs with one to three thorns at leaf nodes. Colorado barberry is 3 to 5 feet tall and typically has two to four main branches; common barberry is up to 9 feet tall and tends to have multiple branches from the base. Colorado barberry's branches are purplish-brown to reddish and so smooth that they look almost shiny; branches of common barberry are grayish and may be ridged or shreddy.

LEAVES: Paddle-shaped leaves grow in small clusters alternating along the stem. Colorado barberry leaves are up to 1¾ inches long; edges may be smooth or may have 3 to 12 spine-tipped teeth. Common barberry leaves are up to 2¼ inches long and have as many as 30 spine-tipped teeth.

FRUIT: Both have glossy oblong red berries that grow in racemes (long clusters of multiple fruits) that droop from leaf axils or branch tips; fruits of both are typically about ⅓ inch long but common barberries may be a bit larger. Clusters of Colorado barberry have 4 to 15 berries; common barberry clusters have 10 to 20 berries. Fruits of both are sour but edible; common barberry has been grown commercially for jam production.

SEASON: Both flower in spring; Colorado barberry continues to flower through midsummer. Fruits ripen in late summer to early fall and may remain on the plants through the next flowering season (as in the photo at right).

COMPARE: Matrimony vine (pg. 152) is a thorny plant with oblong red fruits, but the fruits grow singly or in small groups rather than in racemes.

NOTES: Common barberry is a host for a cereal rust that devastates wheat crops; it has been a target of eradication programs since the 1900s.

green = key identification feature

LARGE SHRUB
OR SMALL TREE

ALTERNATE
COMPOUND
LEAVES

MID TO
LATE SUMMER

Bladder Senna

Colutea arborescens

HABITAT: This fast-growing plant is originally from central and southern Europe and North Africa; it has been planted as an ornamental and has escaped into the wild, where it is occasionally found in rocky, well-drained areas with full sun. It tolerates drought, and grows in scattered spots from the plains through the foothills.

GROWTH: Bladder senna grows as a multi-stemmed leafy shrub or a small tree, typically 5 to 8 feet high and nearly as wide at the top. Older plants may grow taller but are often weedy-looking and leggy, with little growth at the base. Twigs are reddish; older bark is brown. Bright yellow flowers with two wide, wing-like petals and a central keel grow in racemes (long clusters of multiple flowers).

LEAVES: Compound leaves, 3 to 6 inches long, grow alternately. Each leaf has 9 to 13 leaflets on a thin, greenish central stalk. Leaflets are rounded, with a rounded or slightly notched tip and a slightly tapering base; they are ½ to ¾ inch long and two-thirds as wide.

FRUIT: A bladder-like inflated pod, 2¼ to 3 inches long. One long edge of the pod has a distinct but thin raised ridge, while the other appears to be folded inward; the bottom of the pod has a curly thread. Pods are green when young, turning yellowish-green with red tinting at the tips; they eventually turn rosy red. The pods are inedible.

SEASON: Bladder senna in our area flowers from late spring through mid-summer; fruits ripen in mid to late summer, drying out and splitting open to release their seeds in fall.

COMPARE: Bladder senna is a member of the pea (*Fabaceae*) family; many of these plants produce inflated pods. Bladder senna is unusual because it grows much larger than most other *Fabaceae*, and it produces red pods that look like fruit, especially when seen from a distance.

NOTES: Honey made by bees feeding on bladder senna flowers is considered particularly good. The leaves have been used by herbalists to prepare a laxative.

green = key identification feature

LARGE SHRUB
OR SMALL TREE

OPPOSITE
LEAVES

MID TO
LATE SUMMER

Russet

Silver

Buffaloberries (several)

Shepherdia spp.

HABITAT: Two plants with the shared common name of buffaloberry are native to our area. Russet buffaloberry (*Shepherdia canadensis*) inhabits fairly moist, well-drained areas, such as open woods and hillsides. Silver buffaloberry (*S. argentea*) prefers areas that are frequently moist, including streambanks, irrigation ditches and lakeshores. Both grow in the foothills and montane zones; russet buffaloberry extends to the sub-alpine zone.

GROWTH: Multi-branched shrubs or small trees. Russet buffaloberry is less than 8 feet tall; silver buffaloberry is up to 20 feet tall and often forms massive thickets. Russet buffaloberry is thornless; silver buffaloberry branches have long, sharp thorns. Stems of both are rough and scaly; older bark is fissured. Buffaloberry are generally unisexual—a plant is either male or female and each has different flowers; only female plants bear fruit.

LEAVES: Thick leaves up to 2 inches long with rounded tips grow oppositely on short petioles (stemlets). Russet buffaloberry leaves are oval and dark green above, usually with numerous tiny, star-like clusters of white hairs (visible with a lens); undersides are pale and fuzzy, with brownish scales. Silver buffaloberry leaves are narrow and strap-like, with silvery-green tops; undersides are pale silvery-gray.

FRUIT: Juicy oblong to round drupes, ⅛ to ¼ inch long; silver buffaloberries often grow in very dense clusters, while russet buffaloberries are more sparse. Fruits of both have silvery scales and are typically bright red when ripe, occasionally golden. Silver buffaloberry fruits are sweet-tart with a bitter overtone; they are used for jelly. Russet buffaloberry fruits are very bitter and are usually not eaten. There are no toxic look-alikes.

SEASON: Fruits are ripe in mid to late summer and get sweeter after frost.

COMPARE: Roundleaf buffaloberry (*S. rotundifolia*) has rounded, cupped leaves; it grows in semi-desert habitats and in our area is found only in southern Utah. Russian olive (pg. 66) and silverberry (pg. 310) have long, silvery leaves; fruits are yellow or white and are larger, dry and mealy.

NOTES: The fruits contain saponin, a substance that foams like soap.

green = key identification feature

Russet buffaloberry

Silver buffaloberry

LARGE SHRUB
OR SMALL TREE

ALTERNATE
LEAVES

MID TO
LATE SUMMER

Bitter Cherry

Prunus emarginata var. *emarginata*

HABITAT: Bitter cherry grows in cool, moist, rocky areas that receive ample sun. It is found on rocky slopes, in valley bottoms, canyons, and open mixed-wood forests, and alongside streams. It grows from the foothills through the montane zones.

GROWTH: A large spreading native shrub or small tree, bitter cherry can grow to 20 feet in height but is typically 12 feet or shorter. It generally has multiple stems and grows as a thicket; it is also seen as a small tree with a single trunk. Stems are reddish-brown with numerous pale lenticels (breathing pores) and occasional gray patches; old branches are bronze to gray with horizontal orangish lenticels.

LEAVES: Narrowly oval to oval leaves with fine-toothed edges grow alternately on ½-inch petioles (stemlets); one or two small, rounded glands (visible with a lens) are present on the base of the leaf where it joins the petiole. Leaves are 1 to 2½ inches long and generally about one-third as wide; some are quite narrow, only about one-quarter as wide. The tips of the leaves are rounded, and some have a slight inward notch.

FRUIT: Rounded drupes, about ¼ inch across and ½ inch long with a single large pit, grow in small clusters on long, thin stemlets. Fruits are generally red when ripe, but some may become reddish-black. The fruit is edible; it has a fair amount of flesh in proportion to the pit size, but it is very bitter and is generally used to make jam. There are no toxic look-alikes.

SEASON: White flowers appear in late spring to early summer; fruits ripen in mid to late summer.

COMPARE: A larger subspecies of bitter cherry, *P. emarginata* var. *mollis*, grows only in Oregon, Washington and British Columbia; it is more tree-like and can reach 50 feet. Pin cherry (pg. 188) has similar fruits, but its leaves are longer and they have sharply pointed tips.

NOTES: American Indians used the thick bark for basketmaking; the thin outer bark was also used for cordage and as an ornamentation. The bark and roots were used medicinally.

green = key identification feature

LARGE SHRUB
OR SMALL TREE

ALTERNATE
LEAVES

MID TO
LATE SUMMER

American Wild Plum

Prunus americana

HABITAT: This native plum grows in our area in deep, moist soils, and is found in mixed-wood and pinyon-juniper forests (particularly along the edges), shrubby areas in the foothills, thickets on the edges of cultivated or developed areas, and along streams and roads. It produces more fruits when it gets ample sun. It is found from the plains through the foothills zones.

GROWTH: In our area, American wild plum is generally shrub-like and up to 10 feet tall, but it also grows as a densely branching tree up to 25 feet tall with a broad crown. Branches are stiff and dark reddish-brown, with numerous lenticels (breathing pores); many branches are armed with thorns. Older bark is reddish-gray, with a rough texture.

LEAVES: Oval leaves that taper at both ends are 3 to 4 inches long and roughly one-third as wide; they grow alternately on fairly long petioles (stemlets). Edges are finely toothed; the tip is sharply pointed. Leaves are smooth and deep green above, paler below.

FRUIT: A fleshy, egg-shaped to round drupe with an oval pit, usually about 1 inch across. Fruits have a dusty bloom on the surface, and many have a slight vertical cleft. Ripe fruits are bright reddish-orange to pinkish-purple, with juicy, sweet, yellowish flesh. Fruits are edible raw or cooked; tastiness varies from plant to plant. There are no toxic look-alikes.

SEASON: White flowers appear in spring, before the leaves. Fruits ripen from mid through late summer.

COMPARE: Blackthorn (pg. 218) is a thorny related tree, but its leaves are proportionally narrower and its ripe fruit is purplish. Cherry plum (pg. 200) is also related, but it lacks thorns along the branches and its leaves are smaller. Peaches (pg. 78) have somewhat similar fruits, but leaves are much longer and narrower.

NOTES: Plum leaves, stems and pits contain hydrocyanic acid, a cyanide-producing compound. The leaves and pits should never be eaten, and care should be taken to avoid crushing plum pits when juicing the fruits. American plum is the most widely distributed plum in North America.

green = key identification feature

Thorns on trunk

LARGE SHRUB
OR SMALL TREE

ALTERNATE
LEAVES

MID TO
LATE SUMMER

Pin Cherry -OR- Fire Cherry

Prunus pensylvanica

HABITAT: This native cherry grows in sunny, well-drained areas, such as rocky ridges and hillsides, and gravelly areas next to lakes and streams; also found in clearings and edges in mixed-wood and coniferous forests. Pin cherry is one of the first plants to grow after a forest fire. It is found from the plains through the lower montane zones.

GROWTH: In our area, pin cherry typically grows as an arching shrub, 5 to 15 feet high; it can also grow as a small tree up to 25 feet tall. Bark is reddish-brown and smooth, with prominent raised lenticels (breathing pores); bark on older branches often peels off in horizontal strips.

LEAVES: Narrow, sharp-tipped leaves grow alternately from the stems on reddish petioles (stemlets); leaf edges have fine, rounded teeth. Leaves are 3 to 5 inches long, and roughly one-third as wide.

FRUIT: Round, shiny, bright red drupes, about ¼ inch across, grow from reddish stemlets in bunches along the stem. Fruits are translucent when ripe; the large pit can be seen as a shadow in the center of the fruit when the cherries are sunlit. Pin cherries are edible; they're sour when raw but make delicious jelly. There are no toxic look-alikes.

SEASON: Fruits ripen in mid to late summer; the foraging season is usually short because birds relish the cherries and can pick a tree clean of ripe fruit in a short time.

COMPARE: Bitter cherry (pg. 184) has similar fruits, but its leaves are narrower and oval, with a rounded tip. Underripe chokecherries (pg. 270) resemble pin cherries, but the fruits grow in hanging clusters and the leaves are egg-shaped; chokecherries in our area are black when ripe.

NOTES: Pin cherries have a pit that is large in proportion to the flesh, so pitting them for a pie would be a thankless task; they are usually juiced to prepare jelly. Pin cherry leaves and pits contain hydrocyanic acid, a cyanide-producing compound. The leaves and pits should never be eaten, and care should be taken to avoid crushing cherry pits when juicing the fruits. Cooking or drying eliminates the harmful compound.

green = key identification feature

LARGE SHRUB
OR SMALL TREE

ALTERNATE
COMPOUND
LEAVES

LATE
SUMMER

Smooth Sumac

Rhus glabra

HABITAT: Sunny, well-drained areas, such as grasslands, abandoned fields, fencerows and disturbed areas; it is also found along edges and in openings of pinyon-juniper forests. It grows from the plains through the foothills.

GROWTH: This native plant typically grows in our areas as a large shrub, but may also be a small tree up to 15 feet tall. It spreads via rhizomes (underground root-bearing stems) and usually grows in dense colonies. Twigs are smooth and hairless; bark of older stems is dark and smooth with numerous pale lenticels (breathing pores).

LEAVES: Pinnately (feather-like) compound leaves, each with 11 to 31 leaflets, grow alternately. Leaves are 12 to 18 inches long. Leaflets are 2 to 4 inches long and lance-shaped with toothy edges; they are deep green on top, paler underneath. Leaf stalks of smooth sumac are smooth and reddish. Leaves turn red in fall.

FRUIT: Large, cone-shaped clusters of fuzzy, deep red drupes grow upright at the end of the branches, rising above the leaves. The clusters are irregularly shaped; often, two or three clusters of various sizes grow side-by-side at the end of the branch. Clusters are typically 3 to 6 inches long. The drupes are lemony-sour, and can be used to make a lemonade-type beverage. There are no toxic look-alikes with deep red fruits; however, people who are highly allergic to poison ivy, mangoes or cashews should avoid all sumacs, which are in the same family and may cause a severe allergic reaction.

SEASON: Sumac clusters ripen in late summer and persist on the plant through winter, although their flavor is washed away by fall rains.

COMPARE: Littleleaf sumac (*R. microphylla*) is somewhat similar, but it is shorter and its fruiting clusters hang downward along the stems. Its leaves are only 2 to 3 inches long, with 5 to 9 oval, downy leaflets that are less than 1 inch long; the leaf stalks have wing-like extensions between the leaves. In our area, it is found only in central and southern New Mexico.

NOTES: Strain sumac lemonade to remove tiny hairs that irritate the throat.

green = key identification feature

LARGE SHRUB
OR TREE

ALTERNATE
LEAVES

MIDSUMMER
THROUGH
EARLY FALL

*see below

Hawthorns (several)

Crataegus spp.

HABITAT: Eleven native hawthorns, and one non-native, grow in the wild in our area; they hybridize frequently, and identification of exact species is a matter for specialists. Hawthorns inhabit rocky areas, pastures, mixed-wood forests and shelterbelts. Trees in sunny areas produce the most fruit. Hawthorns are most common in the plains and foothills zones.

GROWTH: Small to medium trees or large shrubs; height varies wildly, from 6 feet to over 40 feet. Hawthorns often have a rounded crown and widely spreading branches. Thorns—often long and sharp, as in the photo at right—are always present on native wild hawthorns, but may be negligible or absent on cultivated varieties that have escaped into the wild. Bark on the main trunk is usually dark gray and roughly textured, with vertical fissures; young stems are smooth and gray-brown.

LEAVES: Hawthorn leaves are sharply toothed, although specific shape is variable. The most easily identifiable hawthorns have leaves that are broadly tapered and smooth-edged at the base, with coarse, sharp teeth from the end of the base to the tip. Some species have leaves with distinct lobes; leaves of others are oval and resemble apple leaves, but with larger teeth. Leaves grow alternately, and are typically 2 to 4 inches long.

FRUIT: Pomes, generally oval with slightly flattened sides; they have a projecting floral remnant shaped like a crown on the bottom and grow on a long stemlet. Fruits are generally reddish when ripe, but may be yellowish; size ranges from ¼ to 1 inch across. All hawthorns are edible; see below for a plant with somewhat similar but inedible fruits.

SEASON: Hawthorns ripen from midsummer through early fall.

COMPARE: Ripening cotoneaster fruits (pg. 290) somewhat resemble ripe hawthorns but the leaves are smaller and have very fine teeth, and the base of the fruit has a star-shaped indentation; cotoneasters are inedible.

NOTES: Eating quality varies; taste a few before picking. The best have a fair amount of flesh in proportion to the seeds; flesh may be soft and tender, or crunchy like an apple, and the flavor is often reminiscent of pears.

green = key identification feature   *combined range

Thorns

Thorn

Fleshy hawthorn
(Crataegus succulenta)

LARGE SHRUB OR SMALL TREE   ALTERNATE LEAVES   LATE SUMMER TO EARLY FALL

Pacific Yew

Taxus brevifolia

HABITAT: This native conifer grows as an understory species in cool, moist, well-drained areas such as coniferous forests, ravines, alongside shady streams and the lower parts of slopes. It grows from the plains through the foothills zones.

GROWTH: A very slow-growing tree; young specimens may appear shrub-like. The trunk is often twisted and contorted, and flares out near the base. The outer bark is reddish-brown to gray; it is very thin and flaky, peeling away to expose the reddish-purple inner bark. Branches are reddish-brown; young twigs are green. Very old Pacific yew are up to 60 feet tall; in the shrub form, they are 15 to 20 feet tall. Yews are unisexual; a plant is either male or female, and each bears a different type of flower.

LEAVES: Flat, flexible, dark evergreen leaves with pointed tips grow thickly on the soft green twigs. The leaves are attached alternately in a spiral pattern; the short petiole (stemlet) is parallel to the stem but the leaves bend away from the petiole, growing perpendicular to the twig. Leaves are up to 1 inch long and less than ⅛ inch wide. Undersides are pale, with darker edges and a subtle, darker centerline.

FRUIT: A soft, bright reddish-orange cup called an aril surrounds a single, squarish seed; the aril is about ½ inch wide. Yew arils can be eaten by humans but the seed and all other parts of the plant are dangerously toxic. It's not worth taking the risk; leave the aril alone and let the birds eat the seeds (birds won't be harmed by eating them).

SEASON: Green to bluish-green cone-like structures called strobili develop along the twigs of female plants in early summer; they develop into the arils, which ripen from late summer through early fall.

COMPARE: When the fruits are present, there are no other species in the wild in our region which could be confused with Pacific yew.

NOTES: Yew bark is the source of the anti-cancer drug taxol, and the wood has been used to make archery bows, gunstocks, furniture and decorative items. Both uses deplete native stock of this slow-growing plant.

green = key identification feature

LARGE SHRUB
OR TREE

ALTERNATE
LEAVES

FALL

Netleaf Hackberry

Celtis reticulata

HABITAT: Also called western hackberry, this native tree is fairly adaptable and found in habitats ranging from desert scrub to pinyon-juniper forests to rocky ravines. It grows from the plains through the foothills zones, and is found in semi-desert shrublands.

GROWTH: Netleaf hackberry may grow as a single-trunked tree up to 50 feet tall, but it is frequently a shorter, multi-trunked shrub with many tangled, gnarly branches. Stems are reddish-brown to gray; younger stems are often downy. Bark on the trunk is gray or brownish-gray, with prominent warty bumps and ridges.

LEAVES: Dark green, leathery leaves with a sandpaper-like texture grow alternately on short petioles (stemlets). They are shaped like an elongated heart with a softly pointed or rounded tip. Leaves are 2 to 3 inches long and one-half to one-third as wide; they are widest near the base, which is usually asymmetrical and slightly angled. The veins are net-like and prominent on both surfaces, and are raised on the underside, which is lighter in color than the top side.

FRUIT: Round drupes, ¼ to ⅓ inch in diameter, grow singly or in small groups on long stemlets from leaf axils. They are green in summer, ripening to orangish-red or reddish-brown in fall. The flesh is thin in comparison to the size of the pit; however, it is sweet and delicious. There are no toxic look-alikes that grow on trees.

SEASON: Fruits ripen in fall, and may persist through winter if not consumed by birds.

COMPARE: Common hackberry (pg. 300) is a related tree with similar bark, but its leaves are longer with very long, sharply pointed tips, and lack the prominent veins; its ripe fruits are black.

NOTES: Some sources list this as *C. laevigata* ssp. *reticulata*; under this system, netleaf hackberry is considered a subspecies of sugarberry (*C. laevigata*), a species found mainly in the southeastern U.S.

green = key identification feature

Bark

TREE

ALTERNATE
LEAVES

EARLY TO
MID SUMMER

White Mulberry
Morus alba

HABITAT: White mulberry, originally from China, has been widely planted as an ornamental and has spread into the wild throughout much of North America. It prefers sunny areas and is found in woodlands, fields, urban areas, and along fencelines and road ditches. It is found primarily in the plains zone, but can also grow in the foothills.

GROWTH: Medium to large trees; white mulberry is generally 25 to 40 feet high. Stems are pinkish-brown. Bark of older trees is brown and ridged, with orangish areas between the ridges.

LEAVES: Alternate, with highly variable shape; some have irregular lobes, appearing mitten-like. Leaves are bright green and glossy above with lightly hairy undersides; they are 3 to 5 inches long with rounded teeth.

FRUIT: A multiple fruit up to 1 inch long, composed of numerous drupes originating from a cluster of flowers. A short, soft stemlet remains attached to the picked fruit. Ripe white mulberry fruit may be white, but is more often pink, red or black. Mulberries are soft and sweet, and can be eaten raw or cooked. There are no toxic look-alikes; however, the fruit must be fully ripe and soft before eating, as unripe fruit and all other parts of the plant are mildly toxic.

SEASON: Fruits ripen in early to mid summer.

COMPARE: Texas or littleleaf mulberry (*M. microphylla*) is a related native tree, but its leaves are smaller and densely hairy on the undersides, and its fruits are somewhat sour; in our area, it is found only in southern New Mexico and a few counties of central New Mexico. Red mulberry (*M. rubra*) is another native tree, up to 60 feet tall, with leaves that are hairy underneath and have fine, sharp teeth; it does not grow in our area, being primarily found in the eastern half of the U.S. Both Texas and red mulberry lack the orange areas between the bark ridges.

NOTES: White mulberry leaves are the favored food of the silkworm, and the trees were originally planted in the U.S. during the Colonial days in an attempt to develop a silk-farming industry.

green = key identification feature

Bark

TREE   ALTERNATE LEAVES   LATE SUMMER

Cherry Plum

Prunus cerasifera

HABITAT: Cherry plum is native to Europe and Asia, and has been planted in the U.S. as an ornamental; it has escaped into the wild and is found occasionally in our area. It requires moist, well-drained soil and ample sun, and is found from the plains through the montane zones.

GROWTH: A deciduous, wide-branching tree, generally less than 20 feet tall when found in the wild. The crown is wide, sometimes wider than the height of the tree. Stems and branches are dark reddish-brown, with pale, bumpy lenticels (breathing pores); they are thornless, although some branch tips may have sharp spines. White or pale pink flowers, which are both attractive and very fragrant, blanket the trees in spring before the leaves appear.

LEAVES: Alternate, growing on long, thin petioles. Leaves are 1½ to 2½ inches long and half as wide, with pointed tips and a rounded base; edges have fine, sharp teeth all around. Cherry plum is often grown for its leaves, which turn purplish in late summer; some cultivars have purple leaves year-round. Plants in the wild may have green or purple leaves; plants growing in shade are more likely to have green leaves all season.

FRUIT: A fleshy, rounded drupe, usually less than 1 inch across, with an oval pit. Fruits have a dusty bloom on the surface, and usually have a slight vertical cleft. Ripe fruits are bright reddish-orange to reddish-purple, with juicy, sweet flesh. Fruits are edible raw or cooked; tastiness varies from plant to plant. There are no toxic look-alikes.

SEASON: Fruits are ripe in late summer.

COMPARE: The related American wild plum (pg. 186) may be confused with cherry plum, but American wild plum has sharp thorns and its leaves are up to 4 inches long. Blackthorn (pg. 218) is another thorny relative, but its leaves are proportionally narrower and its ripe fruit is purplish.

NOTES: Plum leaves, stems and pits contain hydrocyanic acid, a cyanide-producing compound. The leaves and pits should never be eaten, and care should be taken to avoid crushing plum pits when juicing the fruits.

green = key identification feature

TREE

ALTERNATE
LEAVES

LATE SUMMER
TO FALL

Apple

Malus pumila

HABITAT: This Asian import is the common grocery-store apple, which may be found in the wild in abandoned orchards and on old homestead sites; they are also found occasionally in areas where apple cores have been discarded by hikers, picnickers, anglers and the like. Apple trees produce more fruit in moderate to full sun, and require adequate moisture. They are found from the plains through the foothills zones.

GROWTH: A sturdy, multi-branched tree, usually with a full, rounded crown. Young branches are downy but smooth and reddish-brown, with numerous lenticels (breathing pores); older bark is rough and gray, often peeling off in scaly patches.

LEAVES: Oval leaves that are coarsely textured grow alternately on long, downy petioles (stemlets); leaves are typically 2 to 3 inches in length and half as wide, with a rounded or tapering base and a pointed tip. Edges have small, sharp teeth. Top sides are dark green; undersides are paler and densely hairy.

FRUIT: The familiar apple is often misshapen and scarred when found in the wild. Ripe fruits are red, yellowish, or yellowish with an overall red blush. The skin is smooth and usually dotted with pale speckles; feral apples often have pockmarks and coarse brown blotches on the skin. They are edible, with no toxic look-alikes; eating quality varies from tree to tree.

SEASON: Apple trees produce fragrant white flowers in spring. Like their domestic forbears, feral apples ripen in late summer to fall.

COMPARE: Related crabapples (*Malus* spp.) grow on similar trees, but the fruits look like tiny apples. They do not generally grow in the wild in our area, although occasional plants may be found near urban areas. Fruits are edible but may have very little flesh in proportion to the seeds. The *Peraphyllum*-family wild crabapple (pg. 156) has similar fruit, but the plants are brushy shrubs with paddle-shaped leaves.

NOTES: If the apple has minor insect damage, simply cut away the affected portion and enjoy the rest of the apple raw or cooked.

green = key identification feature

202 See companion *Cooking with Wild Berries & Fruits of the Rockies* – pg. 8–11

Yellowish feral apples

TENDER
LEAFY PLANT

ALTERNATE
COMPOUND
LEAVES

MID TO
LATE SUMMER

American Spikenard
Aralia racemosa

HABITAT: This native plant is found in the plains zone in rich, open deciduous and mixed-wood forests, thickets, wooded slopes and ravines. It prefers moist, well-drained soil, and grows in full sun to part shade.

GROWTH: A very large, bushy, somewhat top-heavy plant that is almost shrublike and grows from a rhizome (an underground root-bearing stem). Typically 3 to 5 feet in height, with equal width near the top; white flowers grow in numerous long, loose, upright clusters that have an overall conical shape. Stems are soft and greenish-purple, with fine hairs.

LEAVES: Large doubly compound leaves, each with three divisions, grow alternately on the stems; overall leaf length is up to 3 feet. Each of the three divisions has three to five heart-shaped leaflets that are 3 to 6 inches long and two-thirds as wide, with doubly toothed edges and a pointed tip. Leaflets are green and slightly hairy on both surfaces; leaflet nodes are often purplish.

FRUIT: Round drupes, each up to ¼ inch across, replace the flowers in the long, loose clusters (racemes); drupes are greenish when young, ripening to reddish-purple. The effect is that of a long column of tiny grapes. The fruits have a sharp, medicinal taste; some sources list them as edible, while others say they should not be eaten.

SEASON: Spikenard flowers in mid to late summer; fruits ripen from late summer to fall.

COMPARE: Rocky mountain elderberry (pg. 274) is a small shrub with compound leaves and small, dark fruits, but its leaflets are much narrower and its fruits grow in smaller clusters.

NOTES: Like the related sarsaparilla (pg. 246), spikenard has aromatic, spicy-flavored rhizomes that are used as a flavoring agent and can also be eaten when cooked. Young shoot tips can also be cooked as a vegetable.

green = key identification feature

TENDER
VINE

ALTERNATE
LEAVES

LATE
SUMMER

White Bryony

Bryonia alba

HABITAT: This non-native plant is found in the plains zone, in sunny areas with adequate moisture, such as windbreaks, shelterbelts, waste ground and along streams. It is a fast-growing invasive vine that climbs over fences, buildings, rocks, trees and other plants.

GROWTH: Called "the kudzu of the Northwest," white bryony is a tender, perennial vine that can grow as much as 6 inches per day and is often 10 to 12 feet long. Stems are green and slightly angled; they are downy when young, becoming smooth or slightly hairy over the growing season. Long, smooth, unbranched tendrils grow from leaf axils, curling tightly around other plants or supporting structures. Additional stemlets growing from the leaf axils produce clusters of small, yellowish, star-shaped flowers. All parts of the plant cause skin irritation, which may be severe.

LEAVES: Dark green, shiny leaves up to 5 inches across grow alternately on petioles (stemlets) up to 3 inches long. Leaves have 5 to 7 lobes with deep sinuses (the curved depression between the lobes) and several large, coarse teeth. The base of the leaf is deeply notched; lobe tips are sharp. Both surfaces of the leaf are covered with gland-tipped hairs and feel rough to the touch.

FRUIT: Shiny round berries, about ⁵⁄₁₆ inch across, grow in flat-topped clusters; each cluster typically has four to six fruits on short, thin stemlets that grow at the end of a thicker stemlet originating in the leaf axil. Immature fruits are green, ripening to dark purple or purplish-black. They are highly toxic.

SEASON: Fruits ripen in late summer and are eaten by songbirds.

COMPARE: Grapes (pg. 208) have similar leaves and purple fruits, but the fruits are larger and have a dusty bloom, and the vines are woody. Wild cucumber (pg. 36) also has similar leaves; its fruit is a spiny capsule.

NOTES: The dense foliage of white bryony blocks off almost all light from the host plant, weakening and eventually killing it. The root is used in homeopathic medicine to treat back pain and other similar problems.

green = key identification feature

Ripe berries

WOODY
VINE

ALTERNATE
LEAVES

LATE SUMMER
TO EARLY FALL

Riverbank Grape

Vitis riparia

HABITAT: This native vine inhabits moist, rich, sunny areas, including tangles, thickets, cliffs, canyons, river and stream banks and woodland margins. Riverbank grapes are found in the plains and foothills zones.

GROWTH: A straggling, woody vine, up to 50 feet long, that uses coiling tendrils to anchor itself on other plants, fences, poles or buildings. Young stems are greenish and flexible; older stems are reddish-brown or brownish-gray, and usually have shaggy bark.

LEAVES: Toothy leaves, up to 6 inches long, grow alternately from long petioles (stemlets). They have a broad base and three to five lobes, but the lobes may be shallow or deep; teeth are large and coarse. Top sides are dark green and smooth; undersides are pale with small hairs on the major veins.

FRUIT: A tight cluster of edible round, juicy berries hangs from the vine on a sturdy stalk, opposite a leaf; they are ¼ to ½ inch across and are purplish-blue to purplish-black when ripe, with a whitish bloom. Berries grow on short stemlets; each has two to six small, oval seeds. Wild grapes may be confused with several inedible or toxic fruits; see below.

SEASON: Fruits ripen in late summer to early fall.

COMPARE: Canyon grape (*V. arizonica*) is so similar that a non-expert would have a hard time distinguishing it from riverbank grape, but the two plants don't occur in the same locations except for a few New Mexico counties; in our area it is found throughout most of New Mexico and also in southern Utah. Maple-leaf grape (*V. acerifolia*) is a bushier plant, and its leaves are downy; in our area, it is found in a few counties in southeastern Colorado and northeastern Utah. Several plants in our area have round, purplish fruits that are inedible or toxic. For more detail, please see "Be certain, be safe: Wild grapes" on pg. 20–21.

NOTES: All wild grapes are edible; fruits from individual plants may be sour or sweet, regardless of variety.

green = key identification feature

LARGE
WOODY SHRUB

OPPOSITE
LEAVES

EARLY TO
LATE SUMMER

Stretchberry

Forestiera pubescens

HABITAT: This native shrub prefers sunny, moist, well-drained areas and is found along streams, in valleys and canyons, and on hillsides and mesa tops. It grows in the plains and foothills zones, and is found in semi-desert shrublands. It has high heat tolerance.

GROWTH: A multi-branched shrub that often forms dense, interlocked thickets; many branches droop down, making the plant appear **very tangled**. With adequate moisture, it can reach 12 to 15 feet in height. Stems are smooth and pale gray to greenish, with numerous bumpy, light-colored lenticels (breathing pores); older branches are light gray. Branches have numerous **short side branches** that appear spine-like; they grow oppositely, nearly perpendicular to the branch.

LEAVES: Oval to paddle-shaped leaves with short petioles (stemlets) grow oppositely or in small clusters on short spur branches; leaf edges may be smooth or may have fine teeth, especially on the upper half. Leaves are 1 to 2 inches long and half as wide, with rounded or softly pointed tips; top surfaces are shiny and bright green, undersides paler.

FRUIT: Rounded to egg-shaped drupes about ¼ inch long grow in **tight, dense clusters** along the branches, in the axils of the previous year's leaves; the clusters are **tightly pressed against the branches**. Ripe fruits are purplish to bluish-black, with a dusty whitish bloom; most sources consider them inedible.

SEASON: Stretchberry produces masses of yellow flowers in early spring, before the plant leafs out and also before other plants flower; it is sometimes called spring herald for this reason. Fruits ripen from early to late summer and are quickly eaten by birds and small mammals.

COMPARE: The fruits resemble grapes (pg. 208), but grapes are woody vines, not shrubs. Smith's buckthorn (pg. 282) has a similar overall appearance, but its ripe fruits are black and have no bloom.

NOTES: This plant is also called elbow bush because its short, perpendicular side branches appear elbow-like; also called desert olive, due to its habitat.

green = key identification feature

LARGE
WOODY SHRUB

OPPOSITE
COMPOUND
LEAVES

MID TO
LATE SUMMER

Common Elderberry
Sambucus nigra ssp. *canadensis*

HABITAT: This native shrub grows in moist areas such as river and stream banks, woodland edges, shelterbelts, thickets, abandoned fields, roadsides, meadows, and ditch edges. It prefers full sun to part shade, and grows from the plains through the montane zones.

GROWTH: An open shrub, 5 to 12 feet in height, with a broad, rounded crown. Branches are yellowish-gray, with numerous warty lenticels (breathing pores); older bark is yellowish-brown or gray, streaked with white. White flowers grow in large, showy umbrella-like clusters; stemlets are reddish. When the flowers fall and berries are developing, the plant is easy to spot because of the groupings of rounded, reddish-purple flower stemlets, which have a lacy appearance.

LEAVES: Compound leaves, each with 5 to 11 leaflets, grow oppositely on the stem; leaves are 6 to 10 inches long and nearly as wide. Leaflets are 2 to 4 inches long and one-half as wide, broadly oval and tapered on both ends; edges are sharply toothed. The top sides are dark green and smooth; the undersides are paler and may be downy.

FRUIT: Round berries, about ³⁄₁₆ inch in diameter with three to five seeds, grow in drooping, flat-topped clusters (cymes). Berries are green when immature, ripening to deep purple or purplish-black; berry stemlets are reddish-purple. The berries are edible, and are juiced to make jelly, jam and wine. Leaves, stems, seeds and all other parts of all elderberry species are toxic. Common elderberry might be confused with other elderberries whose fruits are generally not eaten; see below.

SEASON: Flowers appear in early summer; fruits ripen in mid to late summer.

COMPARE: Red elderberry (pg. 154) and Rocky Mountain elderberry (pg. 274) have similar growth and leaves, but their fruits grow in rounded clusters rather than flat-topped clusters. Red elderberry's fruits are red when ripe; Rocky Mountain's are black. Blue elderberry (pg. 238) is very similar to common elderberry, but its ripe fruits are blue; they are edible.

NOTES: Some sources list this plant as *S. canadensis*.

green = key identification feature

LARGE
WOODY SHRUB

OPPOSITE
LEAVES

LATE SUMMER
TO EARLY FALL

*see below

Silktassel (several)

Garrya spp.

HABITAT: Two varieties of this non-native plant are found in our area as escapees from cultivation. Both are found in well-drained, rocky locations, such as canyons, rocky hills, dry slopes, scrubby areas, desert grasslands, and in the understory of pinyon-juniper and mixed-wood forests. They grow in the foothills and semi-desert shrubland zones.

GROWTH: Silktassel is an ornamental plant grown for its showy catkins (hanging, downy spikes of flowers). Wright silktassel (*Garrya wrightii*) is an upright woody shrub that may grow to **15 feet in height**, although it is usually shorter when found in the wild; Goldman's silktassel (*G. ovata* ssp. *goldmanii*; also called eggleaf silktassel) is 5 feet or shorter. Both are evergreen, retaining their leaves through winter. Bark is rough and brown. Silktassel plants have **no tendrils**.

LEAVES: Leathery, oval leaves, up to 2 inches long and half as wide, grow oppositely on short petioles (stemlets). Edges are smooth; leaves are yellowish-green and smooth above, paler and hairy below. The opposing leaves, especially those at the ends of branches, tend to fold towards each other like cupped hands.

FRUIT: The slightly egg-shaped to round berries, each ¼ to ⅓ inch long, grow in racemes (long hanging clusters of multiple fruits). They are first green, then reddish, when young, ripening to purplish, purplish-black or bluish-black with a whitish bloom; they eventually turn brown and dry out. They are not considered edible.

SEASON: Silktassel flowers from spring through summer; fruits ripen in late summer to early fall.

COMPARE: Stretchberry (pg. 210) has similar purplish fruits, but its leaves tend to be more paddle-shaped and many grow in clusters on short side branches. Grapes (pg. 208) have somewhat similar fruits, but the leaves are large and very toothy and the plants have tendrils.

NOTES: Silktassel plants contain a bitter, quinine-like substance, making them unappealing as wildlife browse.

green = key identification feature

*combined range

LARGE SHRUB
OR SMALL TREE

ALTERNATE
LEAVES

MID TO
LATE SUMMER

Saskatoon   Utah   Dwarf

Serviceberries (several)

Amelanchier spp.

HABITAT: Three native serviceberry varieties are common in our area; all produce edible fruits that look similar. They are found along streams and lakes; on mountain slopes and hillsides; and in thickets, open woodlands and shaded canyons. Saskatoon serviceberry (*Amelanchier alnifolia;* often referred to simply as saskatoon) and dwarf serviceberry (*A. pumila;* sometimes listed as *A. alnifolia* var. *pumila*) grow from the plains through the montane zones; Utah serviceberry (*A. utahensis*) can be found in similar habitat and zones, but also grows in more arid habitat in semi-desert areas.

GROWTH: Typically shrub-like, but may also appear tree-like. Saskatoons grow to 20 feet tall; Utah and dwarf serviceberries are typically shorter than 10 feet and tend to be bushier. All three have smooth bark that is purplish-red or gray; older bark may be furrowed or splotched with white.

LEAVES: Alternate, with long petioles (stemlets). Leaves are oval with coarse teeth above the midpoint; saskatoon leaves may also have teeth below the midpoint. Saskatoon and dwarf serviceberry leaves are up to 2 inches long, while Utah serviceberry leaves are 1¼ inches or shorter. Saskatoon and Utah serviceberry leaves have up to 13 pairs of veins; dwarf serviceberry leaves have 7 to 9 pairs. Utah serviceberry leaves are typically hairy on both surfaces; dwarf serviceberry leaves are smooth, while saskatoon leaves may be smooth or slightly hairy.

FRUIT: Soft blueberry-like pomes with a crown on the base grow on long stemlets along a fruiting stalk. Saskatoons are up to ½ inch across; Utah and dwarf serviceberries are ⅓ inch or less. Ripe fruits are purplish with a dusty bloom. Saskatoons and dwarf serviceberries are delicious; Utah serviceberries may be bland. There are no toxic look-alikes with a crown.

SEASON: Fruits are ripe from mid to late summer.

COMPARE: Chokecherries (pg. 270) have similar leaves, but fruits lack a crown.

NOTES: Serviceberries got their common name because they flower in early spring, at about the time funeral services were held for people who had died in the winter, when the ground was too frozen to dig.

green = key identification feature

Saskatoon serviceberry

Dwarf serviceberry

LARGE SHRUB
OR SMALL TREE

ALTERNATE
LEAVES

FALL

Blackthorn –OR– Sloe

Prunus spinosa

HABITAT: Originally from the British Isles, Europe and Asia, blackthorn has become naturalized in the Pacific Northwest and now grows in a small part of Idaho. It is found in thickets, drainage ditches and waste ground, and tolerates moist to dry conditions. It grows in the plains through the foothills zones.

GROWTH: A stout-branched, very thorny shrub or small tree, blackthorn can grow to 12 feet in height but is generally shorter. It has a very dense crown that is usually rounded. Branches are brownish to gray and have numerous short spine-tipped branches and long thorns. Older bark is dark gray to blackish, with a rough, scaly texture; wood underneath is orangish. Blackthorn develops suckers and may grow as a thicket.

LEAVES: Oval leaves, ¾ to 1½ inches long and one-third as wide, grow alternately or in small clusters along the stems; leaves have short petioles (stemlets) that are typically brown or reddish. Leaf edges have fine, sharp teeth all around. Young leaves are hairy; older leaves are smooth above with scattered hairs underneath, particularly on the veins.

FRUIT: A rounded drupe with a single, flat pit; fruits are called "sloes." Ripe sloes are purplish to bluish-purple with a dusty bloom; they are ⅓ to ½ inch across and have a small cleft. The flesh is thin and greenish. Fruits are edible but are very astringent, especially when raw; they are generally used to make jam, jelly and sloe gin. There are no toxic look-alikes.

SEASON: Masses of white flowers develop in spring, before the leaves appear. Fruits are ripe in fall; some foragers wait until after a frost to pick the fruits.

COMPARE: American wild plum (pg. 186) is a similar, related plant with thorns, but its leaves are much longer and ripe fruits are red. Cherry plum (pg. 200) is also related, but it lacks thorns, its leaves are proportionally wider and its ripe fruits are red.

NOTES: Blackthorn wood is used to make the famous Irish walking sticks called shillelaghs; the thorns have been used as sewing needles.

green = key identification feature

Large thorn

TENDER
LEAFY PLANT

ALTERNATE
LEAVES

MID TO
LATE SUMMER

Smooth Solomon's Seal

Polygonatum biflorum

HABITAT: Rich, moist mixed-wood and deciduous forests, waste ground, urban areas, roadside ditches, thickets, edges of streams and ponds. It grows from the plains through the foothills zones.

GROWTH: This native plant grows as a single stem in a long arch from a rhizome (an underground root-bearing stem). Smooth Solomon's seal is the largest of the Solomon's seal group of plants, and is often called great Solomon's seal because of its size. The stem can grow up to 5 feet in length, although it is usually much shorter; longer stems arch gracefully, making the plant appear shorter than it is.

LEAVES: Lance-shaped leaves with many parallel veins grow alternately, attached directly to the stem or slightly clasping; leaves are 2 to 7 inches long and are typically narrow. Topsides are green and smooth; undersides are paler, with hairless veins. Leaves are broadest near the base, tapering to a point; edges are smooth and hairless.

FRUIT: Round, dark blue berries, about ⅓ inch across with a slight vertical cleft, grow in small groups or singly from the leaf axils. Berries have a slight bloom, and grow from thin stemlets. They are inedible.

SEASON: Berries mature in mid to late summer.

COMPARE: Clasping-leaved twisted-stalk (pg. 102) has similar leaves, but it is a branching plant and its fruits are red. Starry false Solomon's seal (pg. 106) is shorter and tends to be more upright rather than reclining; its fruits are pumpkin-shaped and grow at the end of the stem. Common false Solomon's seal (pg. 104) also has similar leaves, but it has a cluster of small red fruits that grows at the end of the stem.

NOTES: The rhizome of smooth Solomon's seal is edible when cooked; however, the plant is protected in much of its range and the rhizome should be harvested only where abundant (and legal).

green = key identification feature

Overview of plant

TENDER
LEAFY PLANT

BASAL
LEAF GROWTH

MID TO
LATE SUMMER

Bead Lily –OR– Queen's Cup

Clintonia uniflora

HABITAT: This native wildflower requires moist, cool habitat. It is found as an understory plant in coniferous forests, often along streams; it also grows on cool slopes and on hummocks of decaying wood. Bead lily grows from the plains through the montane zones.

GROWTH: Bright green, glossy leaves grow basally from the underground rhizome (root-bearing stem). A single white flower (rarely two) is borne on a leafless, hairy stalk that rises above the leaves from the center of the plant. Bead lily is generally about 6 inches high.

LEAVES: Smooth, glossy paddle-shaped leaves are up to 6 inches long and one-third as wide; the base is tapered and the tip is broad, ending in a small point. Leaves are deeply cleft by the midrib; edges are smooth, with tiny hairs (visible with a lens). Inconspicuous veins run parallel to the midrib. Each plant typically has two or three leaves, but may have only one.

FRUIT: A single glossy, opaque berry (rarely two) with a deep dimple at the end grows at the end of the leafless stalk, replacing the flower. The berry is a slightly flattened oval, about ⅓ inch across; when ripe, it is bright or deep metallic blue. Fruits are mildly toxic and should not be eaten.

SEASON: Bead lily flowers from late spring through early summer; fruits ripen in mid to late summer.

COMPARE: Lily of the valley (*Convallaria majalis*) is a familiar, cultivated garden plant with similar leaves, but its fruits are red and grow in a raceme (long cluster of multiple fruits).

NOTES: Leaves from young bead lily, picked just as the plants start to flower, are edible, with a delightful, fresh cucumber-like taste. By the time the plants have berries, the leaves are tough and bitter and are generally not eaten. The root is used medicinally as a poultice; birds, including grouse and thrushes, eat the berries.

green = key identification feature

SMALL
WOODY SHRUB

ALTERNATE
COMPOUND
LEAVES

MID TO
LATE SUMMER

Creeping Grape-Holly
–OR– **Oregon Grape**

Mahonia repens

HABITAT: This native plant thrives in partially shaded areas with well-drained acidic soil, especially underneath evergreens and oaks; it also grows in dry, rocky areas. It is found from the foothills through the montane zones.

GROWTH: A creeping, broadleaf evergreen that is generally 6 to 10 inches tall, with slightly greater spread. Plants spread by underground rhizomes (root-bearing stems), and typically form colonies.

LEAVES: Compound leaves, each with three to seven holly-like leaflets, grow alternately; they can be up to 9 inches long but are generally shorter. Leaflets are 1 to 2 inches long and about one-half as wide, with a broad base and a slightly rounded tip; edges have numerous shallow, spine-tipped teeth. Leaflets are shiny and bluish-green on top, whitish and waxy underneath; margins may have a reddish-bronze tint. The terminal leaflet has a long petiole (stemlet); side leaflets are attached directly to the leaf stalk. Leaves turn red in fall.

FRUIT: Round berries, each ¼ to ⅓ inch across, grow in clusters on upright, leafless fruit stalks from the center of the plant; they are purplish-blue with a whitish bloom when ripe. The fruits are thin-fleshed but edible when fully ripe. They are very astringent, but frost increases the natural fructose content, making them somewhat sweeter. They are typically used to make jelly or jam, and are also combined with apple juice to make wine or jelly. There are no toxic look-alikes.

SEASON: Berries mature in mid to late summer and may persist until winter.

COMPARE: Holly-leaved barberry (pg. 240) has similar leaves and fruits, but it is a tall shrub. Fremont's mahonia (pg. 170) is also related, and has similar but smaller holly-like leaves; its fruits are red when ripe.

NOTES: The spiny leaves may cause a rash in sensitive individuals. Some sources list this plant as *Berberis repens*; it also goes by the common name of mahonia.

green = key identification feature

TENDER
VINE

ALTERNATE
LEAVES

MID TO
LATE SUMMER

Blue Ridge Carrionflower
–OR– **Common Smilax**

Smilax lasioneura

HABITAT: This native vine grows in openings in moist, rich deciduous forests; also streambanks, thickets, clearings and waste ground. It is found in the plains and foothills zones.

GROWTH: Common smilax is a vine, up to 8 feet in length. The main stem is greenish to tan. Thin tendrils are present at most leaf axils; the plant uses these to climb over other plants, fences or other structures.

LEAVES: Common smilax has broadly oval or heart-shaped leaves, with several deep parallel veins that have a web of smaller veins between them. They grow alternately on long, pale petioles (stemlets) along the main stem; they are generally 2 to 3 inches long and three-quarters as wide at the base, which is the widest part of the leaf. Leaves are dark green on top, paler and finely hairy underneath; veins on the underside are prominent.

FRUIT: A rounded or ball-shaped cluster of berries on a long, stiff stalk that originates in a leaf axil. Ripe fruits are bluish-black with a whitish bloom. The fruits are generally considered edible but are rubbery and distasteful; they are not eaten.

SEASON: Berries ripen in mid to late summer, and may persist into winter.

COMPARE: The berry cluster may be mistaken for wild grapes (pg. 208); however, the stalk on common smilax makes positive identification easy. Many other *Smilax* species grow in the eastern and southeastern U.S., but common smilax is the only one that grows in our area.

NOTES: Evidently birds (and presumably other wildlife) find the berries as distasteful as humans do; the fruits often remain on the plants well into winter (John F. Thompson and Mary Willson; "Evolution of Temperate Fruit/Bird Interactions: Phenological Strategies," published in *Evolution* 33, 1979).

green = key identification feature

WOODY VINE

ALTERNATE COMPOUND LEAVES

LATE SUMMER TO EARLY FALL

Woodbine

Virginia creeper

Woodbine –AND–
Virginia Creeper

Parthenocissus spp.

HABITAT: These two native vines share similar habitats and are found in rich woodlands, rocky areas and thickets; also in moist areas such as swamp edges and streambanks. They grow in the plains zone.

GROWTH: Woodbine (*Parthenocissus vitacea*) and Virginia creeper (*P. quinquefolia*) are woody vines, up to 70 feet long, that use tendrils to climb over trees, fences and other plants. They are very similar in appearance; one key difference is that the tendrils of woodbine have only one to three branches and are up to 6 inches long, while those of Virginia creeper have up to 10 branches but are less than 2 inches long. Virginia creeper's tendrils have adhesive disks at the end; woodbine's generally don't.

LEAVES: Both species have palmately compound leaves that typically have five oval leaflets. Leaflets are roughly oval with a sharply pointed tip and tapered base; they are up to 4¾ inches long and half as wide. Leaflets of both have sharp teeth on the upper half; the lower half may be toothy or smooth-edged. Leaves are dark green on top, paler below; they grow alternately on long petioles (stemlets) which are smooth on woodbine, hairy on Virginia creeper. In fall, leaves of both turn maroon to bright red.

FRUIT: Round berries grow in loose, open clusters on bright pink stemlets originating from leaf axils. Berries of Virginia creeper are up to ⁵⁄₁₆ inch across; woodbine are up to ⁷⁄₁₆ inch across. Both are deep bluish-purple with a dusty bloom when ripe. Many sources list the berries as toxic; others say they are edible but not tasty. They contain calcium oxalate, which may irritate the throat (Mike Krebill). It's best to avoid them.

SEASON: Berries ripen in late summer to early fall, and may persist on the plant after the leaves drop in the fall.

COMPARE: Berries resemble wild grapes (pg. 208), but the pink berry stemlets and compound leaves distinguish woodbine and Virginia creeper.

NOTES: The berries are eaten by many species of birds.

green = key identification feature

SMALL
WOODY SHRUB

ALTERNATE
LEAVES

MID TO
LATE SUMMER

Dwarf
bilberry

Low
bilberry

Bilberries (several)

Vaccinium spp.

HABITAT: Two native bilberries inhabit our area. Dwarf bilberry (*Vaccinium caespitosum* or *V. cespitosum*) grows from the plains to alpine elevations in rocky meadows, on open slopes and in pine woods. Low bilberry or whortleberry (*V. myrtillus*; sometimes listed as *V. oreophilum*) is found in the montane and sub-alpine zones, where it grows as a groundcover under conifers; it is also found on high ridges and wooded slopes.

GROWTH: Both are low, sprawling woody shrubs less than 1 foot tall that may form extensive colonies; stems are usually flat-sided. Dwarf bilberry stems are reddish-brown; low bilberry's stems are greenish.

LEAVES: Oval leaves grow alternately, attached directly to the stems (sessile); bases are wedge-shaped and tips come to softly rounded points. Dwarf bilberry leaves are ½ to 1¼ inches long; the upper two-thirds of the leaf has small, rounded teeth tipped with minute glands. Low bilberry leaves are ⅓ to 1½ inches long and have fine teeth all around.

FRUIT: Rounded berries, ¼ to ⅓ inch across, grow singly on short stemlets from leaf axils; the base is flattened and has a circular depression. The surface has a dusty bloom; pulp inside the berry is reddish or purplish. Dwarf bilberries are bright blue to bluish-black; low bilberries are bluish-black or reddish-purple. Both are delicious; they can be eaten raw but are usually used for jam and baked goods. There are no toxic look-alikes.

SEASON: Fruits are ripe in mid to late summer.

COMPARE: Grouse whortleberry (pg. 144) looks similar to low bilberry, but its leaves are half the size; its ripe fruit is red and much smaller. Bog blueberry (*V. uliginosum*) is found scattered throughout the northern half of our area; its leaves have no teeth, its fruits grow in small clusters rather than singly and the base of the berry has a distinct crown.

NOTES: Bilberries resemble grocery-store blueberries (generally highbush blueberry, *V. corymbosum*, which is not native to our area), but the pulp of blueberries is greenish and fruits grow in clusters rather than singly. Bilberry extract is marketed as a health tonic.

green = key identification feature

Base of berry

Dwarf bilberry

Low bilberry

EDIBLE

SMALL
WOODY SHRUB

ALTERNATE
LEAVES

MID TO
LATE SUMMER

Trailing
black

Wolf's

Trailing Black Currant –AND– Wolf's Currant

Ribes spp.

HABITAT: These two similar-appearing native currants inhabit damp areas such as streambanks, wet meadows and moist forests. Trailing black currant (*Ribes laxiflorum*; also called *R. coloradense*) prefers sunny, open woodlands, while Wolf's currant (*R. wolfii*) is found in rocky, shaded woodlands (Al Schneider, Southwest Colorado Wildflowers). Trailing black currant grows from the plains through the montane zones; Wolf's currant is found from the montane through the sub-alpine zones.

GROWTH: Both species commonly grow as spreading, ground-hugging plants, often appearing no taller than 3 feet, but they may also be seen as taller, upright shrubs up to 6 feet high; trailing black currant may also gain height by climbing over other plants. Twigs are green and downy, becoming hairless as they mature; older branches of trailing black currant are reddish-brown, while Wolf's are gray. Stems have no prickles or thorns.

LEAVES: Somewhat wrinkly, deeply veined leaves with five distinct lobes and coarse, rounded teeth grow alternately on long, hairy petioles (stemlets). Leaves of Wolf's currant are ¾ to 2¼ inches long, while those of trailing black currant are up to 4½ inches long.

FRUIT: Rounded berries approximately ⅓ inch long grow in racemes (long clusters of multiple fruits); a dried flower remnant is present at the end of the berry. Fruits of both are bluish or bluish-black, generally with a heavy bloom that makes them look dull blue; they are covered with short, bristle-like glands. They are edible but may be dry or bitter, although some foragers report that trailing black currants are often quite good (Al Schneider). There are no toxic look-alikes.

SEASON: Fruits ripen from mid to late summer.

COMPARE: Sticky currant (pg. 278) has similar bristly berries, but the berries are black when ripe and its leaves are very sticky on both surfaces.

NOTES: Birds are fond of the berries of trailing black currant.

green = key identification feature

Trailing black currant, flowering

Wolf's currant fruits

SMALL
WOODY SHRUB

ALTERNATE
LEAVES

LATE
SUMMER

Common Juniper

Juniperus communis

HABITAT: Dry, sunny openings in coniferous and mixed-wood forests; also found on rocky outcrops, ridges and exposed slopes. It grows from the plains through the sub-alpine zones.

GROWTH: In our area, common juniper is a sprawling evergreen shrub, up to 4 feet in height, with short branches that tend to grow upright. It can also grow as a tree, but that form is not generally found in our area. Bark is reddish-brown, fibrous and shreddy. Common juniper is unisexual—a plant is either male or female, and each produces a different type of flower.

LEAVES: Narrow, pointed, awl-like evergreen needles, about ½ inch long, grow alternately in clusters of three; they have a strong smell which is both piney and resinous. Needles are concave on top, with a whitish center; undersides are dark green. Except near the tip of the branch, needles usually grow almost perpendicular to the branches, giving each branch a bushy appearance.

FRUIT: The fruits, borne on female plants, are round, berry-like cones, about ⅓ inch across, which grow on short stemlets or are connected directly to the branch. Cones are bluish-white with a waxy bloom; they are usually profuse. When crushed, they smell like gin. The cones are used as a seasoning.

SEASON: Fruits ripen in late summer and usually persist through winter.

COMPARE: Creeping juniper (*J. horizontalis*) is a low-growing juniper with similar-looking dusty blue, rounded fruits, but its leaves appear scaly like those of Rocky Mountain juniper (pg. 244); although its fruits are similar in appearance to common juniper, they are not edible. In our area, creeping juniper is found in western Wyoming and much of Montana.

NOTES: Common juniper is the most widespread conifer in the world. It is native to the United States and Canada, as well as Eurasia, Japan, Croatia and Sweden; it typically grows as a columnar tree in areas other than North America, although the tree form is found in New England. The cones of common juniper are used to flavor gin.

green = key identification feature

Juniper growing under
lodgepole pine

LARGE
WOODY SHRUB

OPPOSITE
LEAVES

LATE SPRING
TO EARLY
SUMMER

DELICIOUS

Sweetberry Honeysuckle

Lonicera caerulea

HABITAT: Several cultivars of this plant, also called honeyberry or Russian blue honeysuckle, are grown commercially in Canada as well as in test plantings in Oregon and Idaho. *Lonicera caerulea* is also listed by the USDA as a native species; plants encountered in the wild may be native plants or escaped cultivars. Sweetberry honeysuckle prefers moist, well-drained areas such as streambanks, and tolerates both partial shade and full sun; it is found from the foothills through the montane zones.

GROWTH: A deciduous, cold-tolerant shrub that is usually 3 to 6 feet tall. Depending on the cultivar, the form is variable; some grow in a very upright fashion, but other specimens have drooping branches. Twigs are reddish to brownish and hairy when young. Bark of older stems is brownish or grayish and peels off in lengthwise strips.

LEAVES: Oval to egg-shaped leaves, 1¼ to 3 inches long and one-third to one-half as wide, grow oppositely on short petioles (stemlets) that are often reddish. Edges have fine hairs (visible with a lens). Leaf surfaces may be smooth or slightly hairy; tips are rounded or softly pointed.

FRUIT: Sweetberry honeysuckle fruits are bright or deep blue berries with a dusty bloom; occasionally, berries have a reddish tint. Shape is variable, depending on the cultivar. Some are nearly 1 inch long and shaped like an elongated bell without the flare at the bottom; the base may be open or closed in this form. Others are oval or barrel-shaped; in a form that is sometimes called mountain fly honeysuckle, the berries grow as paired, bullet-shaped fruits joined at the base. All are edible and juicy, with soft seeds that don't need to be removed. The berries are tart to sweet-tart, and are usually used for jam, sauces or baked goods rather than out-of-hand eating. There are no toxic look-alikes.

SEASON: Berries are ripe in late spring to early summer.

COMPARE: Nothing resembles sweetberry honeysuckle when in fruit.

NOTES: Haskap is a cultivar developed at the University of Saskatchewan; it is the most common variety in commercial production.

green = key identification feature

LARGE
WOODY SHRUB

OPPOSITE
COMPOUND
LEAVES

MID TO
LATE SUMMER

Blue Elderberry

Sambucus nigra ssp. *caerulea*

HABITAT: This native shrub grows in moist, well-drained areas, such as river and stream banks, forest openings and edges, thickets, grasslands, roadsides, and at the bases of canyons and cliffs. It prefers full sun to partial shade, and is found from the plains through the sub-alpine zones.

GROWTH: A leafy shrub, up to 20 feet in height but usually shorter, with a broad, rounded crown; it often forms a thicket. Young branches are smooth and light green. Stems are gray or brownish, and rough-textured with numerous bumpy lenticels (breathing pores); older stems and the trunk are often deeply furrowed. White flowers grow at the ends of the stems in large, showy umbrella-like clusters.

LEAVES: Compound leaves, each with five to nine leaflets, grow oppositely on the stem on long, grooved petioles (stemlets); leaves are 5 to 8 inches long and nearly as wide. Leaflets are up to 4 inches long and one-third to one-quarter as wide, oval to lance-shaped with toothy edges; tips are sharply pointed and bases are often asymmetrical. The top sides are dark green and smooth; undersides are paler and may be downy.

FRUIT: Round berries, about ³⁄₁₆ inch in diameter with several seeds, grow in drooping, flat-topped clusters; they are green when immature. When ripe, most are blue with a waxy, whitish bloom, but some berries, even in the same cluster, may lack the waxy bloom and appear black. Berry stemlets often turn reddish-burgundy as the fruit ripens. Fully ripe berries are edible; leaves, stems and unripe berries are toxic.

SEASON: Flowers appear in late spring to early summer; fruits ripen in mid to late summer.

COMPARE: Common elderberry (pg. 212) is a similar plant whose ripe berries are purplish-black; like blue elderberry, its berries ripen in mid to late summer and are edible. Red elderberry (pg. 154) may be as tall as blue elderberry, but its ripe fruits are bright red, and ripen in early to mid summer; its berries are generally regarded as inedible.

NOTES: The berries are usually juiced to make jelly, jam or wine.

green = key identification feature

LARGE
WOODY SHRUB

ALTERNATE
COMPOUND
LEAVES

LATE
SUMMER

Holly-Leaved Barberry

Mahonia aquifolium

HABITAT: This native shrub prefers cool, well-drained areas with dappled shade and shelter from winter winds. It is found in rocky forests and on shaded hillsides and sagebrush flats. It grows from the plains through the foothills, and may grow in protected areas of semi-desert shrublands.

GROWTH: An upright evergreen shrub that may grow to 8 feet in height. Stems are generally stiff and upright, and are typically unbranched. Bark is reddish-brown and often has numerous bumps and rough patches from previous years' growth. In spring, bright yellow flowers grow in large clusters at the stem tips, and in smaller clusters along the stems.

LEAVES: Compound leaves, each with five to nine holly-like leaflets, grow alternately; they are 6 to 12 inches long. Leaflets are 2 to 3 inches long and about one-half as wide, with a broad base and a pointed tip; edges have numerous shallow, spine-tipped teeth. Leaflets are shiny and bluish-green on top, whitish and waxy underneath; margins may have a reddish-bronze tint. The terminal leaflet has a long, thin petiole (stemlet); side leaflets are attached directly to the leaf stalk. Leaves turn red in fall.

FRUIT: Round berries, each ¼ to ⅓ inch across, grow in clusters at stem tips or along the stems; they are purplish-blue with a whitish bloom when ripe. The fruits are thin-fleshed but edible when fully ripe. They are very astringent, but frost increases the natural fructose content, making them somewhat sweeter. They are typically used for jam, or juiced to make jelly or other sweetened products. There are no toxic look-alikes.

SEASON: Berries mature in late summer and may persist until winter.

COMPARE: Creeping grape-holly (pg. 224) has similar leaves and fruits, but it is a very short shrub. Fremont's mahonia (pg. 170) is also related and has similar but smaller holly-like leaves; its fruits are red when ripe.

NOTES: Some sources list this plant as *Berberis aquifolium*. It is the state flower of Oregon, and another common name for it is tall Oregon grape. The flowers are edible raw, and can also be steeped in boiling water to make a lemony drink.

green = key identification feature

LARGE
WOODY SHRUB

ALTERNATE
LEAVES

LATE SUMMER
THROUGH
EARLY FALL

Lotebush

Ziziphus obtusifolia var. *canescens*

HABITAT: This native shrub is a desert plant that grows best in hot, dry areas. It is found on desert flats, mesa tops, canyon slopes and rocky hillsides, and in grasslands and scrubby areas. It grows in the plains and semi-desert shrubland zones.

GROWTH: A twisted, stiff-branched shrub up to 10 feet tall whose numerous branches cross each other and zigzag, giving the plant an unkempt, irregular look. Young stems have a whitish or gray waxy coating that makes them appear gray to greenish-gray; they are well armed with sharp, thick, curved thorns up to 3 inches long, giving the plant the alternate common name of graythorn. Older stems are light gray.

LEAVES: Thick, oblong leaves, typically about ¾ inch long and one-quarter to one-third as wide, grow alternately or in small clusters along the branches. Leaves are dull green and downy; they have a short, thick petiole (stemlet) and a rounded tip that may have a slight inward notch. The midrib is deep and the leaf is often folded slightly inward. The leaves fall off the plants in early fall or during periods of drought, leaving behind a twisted, thorny mass of gray branches.

FRUIT: Oval, dark blue to bluish-black drupes, ¼ to ⅓ inch long with a whitish bloom, grow in small groups from leaf axils and at branch tips. The fruits are dry and mealy; they are edible but not palatable.

SEASON: Fruits ripen from late summer through early fall.

COMPARE: Javelina bush (pg. 148) is a thorny, multi-branched shrub, but it is a shorter shrub whose stems lack the whitish waxy coating; its ripe fruits are football-shaped and red. Warnock's snakewood (pg. 284) is also a thorny, multi-branched shrub whose branches also lack the waxy coating; its leaves are paddle-shaped and its ripe fruits are round and glossy black.

NOTES: Some sources list this plant as *Condalia lycioides*. Birds build their nests in the thorny plants to get protection from predators; quail and doves eat the fruits.

green = key identification feature

TREE

ALTERNATE
LEAVES

LATE
SUMMER

Rocky
Mountain

Utah

Rocky Mountain Juniper –AND–
Utah Juniper

Juniperus spp.

HABITAT: These two native evergreens are found in open, dry, rocky areas, such as ridgetops, plateaus and hilltops. Utah juniper (*Juniperus osteo-sperma*; also listed as *J. utahensis*) grows in semi-desert shrublands through the foothills zones; Rocky Mountain juniper (*J. scopulorum*) is found in the same areas as well as in the montane zone.

GROWTH: Both are short trees, 30 feet tall or less. Rocky Mountain juniper has more dense foliage and an overall triangular shape, while Utah juniper is more open with a twisted trunk and an irregular shape. Bark is thin and shreds off in vertical strips. Junipers are usually unisexual—a plant is either male or female, and each produces a different type of flower.

LEAVES: Twigs of both trees have tiny scale-like leaves which grow together so closely that the trees appear to have flat-sided, grayish-green scaly twigs; Rocky Mountain juniper's leaves are slightly smaller, giving the branches a more delicate appearance. Young trees and new growth have pointed, awl-like needles. The foliage has a strong, piney smell.

FRUIT: The fruits, borne on female trees, are round, berry-like cones that grow at the tips of scale-covered branches; cones of Rocky mountain juniper are about ¼ inch across, while Utah juniper's cones are up to ½ inch. Cones of both are bluish, with a waxy bloom; they are used as a seasoning.

SEASON: Cones mature in late summer and persist through winter.

COMPARE: Several trees in our area have similar scale-like leaves. Bark of alligator juniper (*J. deppeana*) is broken into raised, rectangular plates; in our area it grows only in New Mexico. Oneseed juniper (*J. monosperma*) may appear to have multiple trunks because its branches begin growing low on the trunk, close to the ground; in our area, it is found throughout New Mexico, in southern Utah and in parts of Colorado. Arizona cypress (*Cupressus arizonica*) is a tall, narrow tree whose cones are brownish.

NOTES: Junipers provide food and cover for birds and other wildlife.

green = key identification feature

Rocky mountain juniper

Utah juniper

Rocky mountain juniper

TENDER
LEAFY PLANT

SINGLE
COMPOUND
LEAF

MIDSUMMER

Sarsaparilla

Aralia nudicaulis

HABITAT: Rich, moist, sun-dappled mixed-wood and hardwood forests; thickets and prairie areas; occasionally near streams and bogs. It grows in the plains and foothills zones.

GROWTH: This native plant has a single, three-stemmed, doubly compound leaf growing from a rhizome (an underground root-bearing stem) at the top of a long, erect, hairless leaf stalk; total height may be as much as 2 feet, but it is usually shorter. The flowering/fruiting stalk is separate, rising from the same point as the leaf stalk; it is shorter, typically 5 to 8 inches in height.

LEAVES: Three-part, doubly compound; each of the three leaf stalks has three to five oblong, toothy leaflets with rounded bases and pointed tips. Leaflets are 2 to 4 inches long and about two-thirds as wide; they are broadest at or below the midpoint.

FRUIT: The leafless fruiting stalk divides into three stemlets (occasionally two); each is topped with a rounded cluster of black berries on slender stemlets that emanate from a central point, much like the fluffy head of a dandelion gone to seed. Berries are round and about ⅛ inch in diameter. They are inedible when raw; although they may be edible when cooked, sources disagree on this, so they are best left to the birds, foxes and bears, who consume them with no ill effects.

SEASON: Fruits ripen in midsummer.

COMPARE: With its distinctive trio of fruiting clusters and its three-part leaf, sarsaparilla resembles nothing else in our area when it is fruiting.

NOTES: The underground rhizome is very fragrant, and has been used to make tea and other beverages. It is not, however, the source of the flavoring in root beer and the soft drink called sarsaparilla; rather, that flavor traditionally came from the roots and bark of the unrelated sassafras tree (*Sassafras albidum*), a plant which grows in the eastern and southeastern U.S. but not in our area.

green = key identification feature

TENDER
LEAFY PLANT

WHORLED
LEAVES

MID TO
LATE SUMMER

Dyer's Madder

Rubia tinctorum

HABITAT: An introduced plant that grows in the semi-desert shrubland zone, dyer's madder is found in sunny, well-drained locations, alongside paths, on waste ground and in scrubby areas.

GROWTH: Dyer's madder is a perennial whose main stems are up to 8 feet long; rather than growing upright, the stems sprawl along the ground or over rocks in vine-like fashion. Stems are stout, yellowish to greenish and ribbed; the edges of the ribs have short prickles, which may help the plant to climb. Smaller secondary stems branch from the main stem at leaf axils. Three long flower stalks grow at the end of the secondary stems; each stalk is crowned with a rounded cluster of yellow flowers that develop into fruits.

LEAVES: Lance-shaped leaves grow in whorls of four to six leaves; the whorls grow at regular intervals along the stems. Leaves are 1½ to 3¾ inches long and about one-quarter as wide; they have very short petioles (stemlets) and are tapered on both ends. They are light yellowish-green and have scattered fine, white hairs; edges are finely toothed. The mid-ribs on leaf undersides have small prickles.

FRUIT: Smooth, glossy rounded berries, about ⅛ inch across, grow on short stemlets in an open, rounded cluster at the end of each flower stalk. Berries are green when immature, turning deep red, reddish purple and, finally, black; the various colors may all be present at the same time. The berries are not edible.

SEASON: Berries ripen gradually from mid to late summer.

COMPARE: The whorls of leaves on long stems, and the clusters of flowers or berries at the ends of the three stemlets, make it difficult to confuse this plant with any other.

NOTES: Dried, ground rhizomes (root-bearing stems) of dyer's madder have been used for centuries to produce deep red or orange dyes.

green = key identification feature

Ripe berries

TENDER
LEAFY PLANT

ALTERNATE
LEAVES

MIDSUMMER
TO EARLY FALL

Eastern
black

Hoe

Eastern Black Nightshade
–AND– Hoe Nightshade

Solanum spp.

HABITAT: These two weedy plants grow in the plains zone, in agricultural areas, waste ground, urban areas, thickets and woodland openings. They prefer partial to full sun, and can adapt to moist or dry conditions.

GROWTH: Eastern black nightshade (*Solanum ptycanthum*) is a native plant; hoe nightshade (*S. physalifolium*) is an introduced species. Both are typically 12 to 24 inches tall and branch multiple times. Young stems are green and round, becoming brownish and woody over the season.

LEAVES: Alternate, on flattened petioles (stemlets). Shape is inconsistent; in general, they are triangular to elliptic, but edges may be smooth and wavy, or may have wide, blunt teeth. Leaves are up to 3 inches long and two-thirds as wide, although leaves near the ends of the branches are smaller. Hoe nightshade leaves are covered with fine, short hairs on both surfaces; leaves of eastern black nightshade are only slightly hairy.

FRUIT: Round, juicy berries, about ⅓ inch in diameter with a star-shaped cap, grow in small hanging clusters. Young berries of both species are green; Eastern nightshade ripens to deep, glossy black, while hoe nightshade is purplish-green to brownish when ripe. *Underripe berries are toxic.* Some foragers eat fully ripe eastern black nightshade berries in small quantities, but even this may cause intestinal problems in some people. Hoe nightshade are generally regarded as mildly toxic even when ripe. To avoid potential problems, simply consider both types inedible.

SEASON: Small, white, star-shaped flowers grow throughout summer; berries follow, ripening throughout midsummer and into early fall.

COMPARE: Climbing nightshade (pg. 124) grows as a vine; its fruits are red when ripe and its flowers are purple. Silverleaf nightshade (pg. 58) has yellowish fruits and silvery leaves.

NOTES: For more information on judging ripeness and eating eastern black nightshade berries, consult *Nature's Garden* (Sam Thayer).

green = key identification feature

Eastern black nightshade

SMALL
WOODY SHRUB

ALTERNATE
COMPOUND
LEAVES

MID TO
LATE SUMMER

Trailing Blackberry

Rubus ursinus

HABITAT: This native plant grows in open areas, including prairies, clearings, waste ground and logged or burned areas; it is also found in shady areas such as forests. Although it will grow in dry soil, it prefers areas with ample moisture and may be found in locations such as river islands and lakeshores that experience seasonal flooding. Primarily a low-elevation plant, it is found from the plains through the foothills, although it does grow in some lower montane-zone canyons.

GROWTH: As its name suggests, trailing blackberry is a trailing, low-growing vine-like shrub; like other similar members of the *Rubus* group, this plant is often called a dewberry. Stems are woody but weak, usually sprawling along the ground in a tangle rather than rising erect; the tips often develop roots where they touch the ground. Stems are thin and round, with numerous weak, thin rounded prickles that break off easily. Young stems are greenish to reddish, with a whitish waxy bloom.

LEAVES: The compound leaves grow alternately on long petioles (stemlets) that have scattered thin prickles. Leaves of fruiting stems have three leaflets, while those of non-fruiting stems typically have five. Leaflets are up to 3 inches long; edges are toothy and may be somewhat lobed.

FRUIT: A compound drupe, about ⅜ inch across and somewhat longer; it may appear conical. Fruits are green and hard at first, turning from bright red to burgundy to purplish before ripening to glossy black; the core typically remains in the picked fruit. The fruits are juicy and sweet, and are highly prized for baking and jam-making. There are no toxic look-alikes.

SEASON: Fruits ripen in mid to late summer.

COMPARE: Himalayan blackberry (pg. 286) has similar but larger fruits, and the plant is much taller and bushier. Its stems lack the powdery coating; they are ridged or grooved rather than round, and have large, flat, wide-based thorns.

NOTES: Some sources refer to this plant as California or Pacific blackberry. Marionberries are a hybrid bred from the trailing blackberry.

green = key identification feature

Stem closeup

SMALL
WOODY SHRUB

ALTERNATE
COMPOUND
LEAVES

MID TO
LATE SUMMER

Whitebark Raspberry

Rubus leucodermis

HABITAT: This native shrub prefers sun-dappled, moist areas, and is found in pine or mixed-conifer forests, particularly along edges and in openings; also grows in fields and disturbed areas, and on open hillsides. It is found from the plains through the sub-alpine zones.

GROWTH: Whitebark raspberries are brambles, sprawling vine-like shrubs that form a thicket. Stems, called canes, are up to 6 feet long and usually arch but may be upright; canes that arch will root where they touch the ground. The canes are round and have curved, flattened thorns. A heavy white bloom covers the canes, giving the plant its common name.

LEAVES: Compound, toothy leaves with sharply pointed tips grow alternately on the canes. Leaves usually have three leaflets, but may have five; leaflets are up to 2½ inches long, and some may be slightly lobed. The terminal leaflet has a long petiole (stemlet); side leaflets have very short petioles, appearing at times to attach directly to the leaf stalk. Leaves are green above, and whitish beneath, with fine, soft hairs.

FRUIT: A compound drupe, up to ½ inch across. Fruits are green and hard at first, progressing from yellowish-orange to bright red to wine-red before ripening to blackish-purple, giving the plant its other common name, black-cap. Ripe fruits detach cleanly from the plant, leaving the receptacle (core) behind; the picked fruit is hollow. Fruits are edible and delicious, raw or cooked; when ripe, there are no toxic look-alikes.

SEASON: Fruits ripen in mid to late summer.

COMPARE: Black raspberry (*R. occidentalis*) is very similar, but older stems are purplish. It is found is the eastern half of the U.S. and Canada but rarely if ever grows in our area. Blackberries (pgs. 252, 286) have similar growth habits and a compound fruit that is black at maturity, but the receptacle (core) stays with the berry when it's picked. Red raspberries (pg. 138) look similar to underripe whitebark raspberries; however, red raspberry canes are prickly but not thorny, and lack the white bloom.

NOTES: The leaves make a fine tea; use unwilted leaves to avoid problems.

green = key identification feature

SMALL
WOODY SHRUB

ALTERNATE
LEAVES

MID TO
LATE SUMMER

American

Northern

American Black Currant –AND–
Northern Black Currant

Ribes spp.

HABITAT: These very similar, related native shrubs grow in moist areas such as rich woodlands, swamps, ravines, canyons and streambanks. American black currants are found from the plains through the foothills; the range of northern black currants extends through the montane zone.

GROWTH: Both are erect shrubs that are 3 to 5 feet tall; stems have no prickles or thorns. Stems of American black currant (*Ribes americanum*) are squarish in cross-section, with distinct ridges; stems of northern black currant (*R. hudsonianum*) are round and smooth.

LEAVES: Somewhat wrinkly, deeply veined leaves with coarse, rounded teeth on the edges grow alternately, singly or in small clusters on long, thin petioles (stemlets). Each leaf has three to five distinct lobes, resembling a maple leaf with rounded teeth. American black currant leaves are up to 2¾ inches long and have tiny yellow resin dots (visible with a lens) on both surfaces; those of northern black currant are up to 4¾ inches long and have resin dots on the underside only.

FRUIT: Round ¼- to ⅜-inch berries grow in a raceme (a long cluster of multiple fruits); a prominent flower remnant, often called a pigtail, is present at the end of the berry. The raceme may point upwards on northern black currant, or may droop with the weight of the fruit; racemes of American black currant hang downward. Immature berries are green, turning red before ripening to black. Northern black currant berries are covered with resin dots; they are unpalatable but can be eaten safely. American black currant berries are delicious, and can be eaten raw, used in baking, or cooked into jelly, jam and other dishes. There are no toxic look-alikes.

SEASON: Both types of currants are ripe from mid to late summer.

COMPARE: Several other currants with black fruits grow in our area; please see pgs. 262, 278 and 280 for descriptions

NOTES: All parts of northern black currant have a foul odor when crushed.

green = key identification feature

American black currant

SMALL
WOODY SHRUB

ALTERNATE
LEAVES

LATE SUMMER
TO EARLY FALL

Alder-Leaved Buckthorn
Rhamnus alnifolia

HABITAT: Moist areas, including mixed-wood forests, damp meadows, swampy areas, streambanks and thickets. Sometimes found growing on the wet edge of a pond or lake. It grows from the plains through the foothills zones.

GROWTH: A short, upright shrub, 3 feet or less in height with equal spread. Branches fork several times. Twigs are smooth and reddish or brownish; young branches are downy. It may form colonies, with many short shrubs in a tight group. Alder-leaved buckthorn is usually unisexual—a plant is either male or female, and each produces a different type of flower.

LEAVES: Roughly oval, with a sharp tip; each has six to eight pairs of deep, gently curving veins. Leaves are up to 4 inches long and one-half as wide; they grow alternately from the stems on short, smooth petioles (stemlets). Edges are finely toothed; both surfaces are smooth and somewhat glossy, although the veins may be slightly hairy on the underside. Tiny paired, leaf-like appendages called stipules grow at the base of each leaf petiole where it joins the main stem.

FRUIT: Glossy round drupes, about ¼ inch in diameter, are red when under-ripe, turning black when ripe. Fruits grow on thin stemlets from the leaf axils of female plants. The fruits are inedible.

SEASON: Fruits are red in late summer, turning black by early fall.

COMPARE: Common buckthorn (pg. 292) is a taller, related shrub found in drier habitat; its leaves are more egg-shaped. Glossy buckthorn (pg. 294) is also taller; it has smooth-edged leaves, and leaf undersides are hairy.

NOTES: Unlike common buckthorn and glossy buckthorn, alder-leaved buckthorn is a native plant; it is not considered invasive, and can sometimes be hard to find. It is a favored late-summer food of black bears.

green = key identification feature

LARGE
WOODY SHRUB

OPPOSITE
LEAVES

SUMMER

Twinberry Honeysuckle
Lonicera involucrata

HABITAT: In the wild, this native shrub is typically found in areas with ample moisture, such as moist woods, along streambanks and swamp edges and near bogs. It tolerates light shade, but produces more fruit in areas with ample sun. In the northern part of our area it grows at low to montane elevations; in the warmer southern part of our region, it is more frequently found in the sub-alpine zone.

GROWTH: Twinberry is an open, multi-branched upright shrub, typically 6 to 10 feet tall; its form is vase-like, and the top can be almost as wide as the plant is tall. Young stems are yellowish, turning yellowish-brown as they mature; the trunk is gray and shreddy. Small tubular flowers grow on long stemlets from leaf axils, usually in pairs. Twinberry may form thickets.

LEAVES: Opposite, elliptic leaves with a short petiole (stemlet) are generally 1 to 5 inches long and one-half to two-thirds as wide; tips are pointed or slightly rounded. Edges are untoothed and have fine hairs (visible with a lens); leaves are smooth and glossy above and usually lightly hairy below. The veins and midrib are distinct, especially underneath.

FRUIT: Glossy, rounded black berries, ¼ to ⅓ inch across, typically grow in pairs on long stemlets which are often reddish. Deep reddish bracts grow at the base of the fruit, often pointing backwards; the bracts are frequently wavy and resemble a frilly skirt. These showy bracts account for another of the plant's common names, bracted honeysuckle. Some sources list the berries as edible but very bitter and unpalatable, while others list them as mildly toxic. It is best to consider them inedible.

SEASON: Twinberry's yellow, orange or reddish flowers bloom from spring through summer; fruits ripen throughout the summer.

COMPARE: Some bush honeysuckles (pgs. 160, 164) have a similar form and leaves, but berries are orange or red and have no red bracts at the base.

NOTES: The bark and leaves were used medicinally by American Indians; fruits were crushed to produce a purple or black dye. The flowers attract hummingbirds and butterflies; bears and birds eat the berries.

green = key identification feature

Closeup of berries

LARGE
WOODY SHRUB

ALTERNATE
LEAVES

MID TO
LATE SUMMER

Golden Currant

Ribes aureum

HABITAT: This native shrub prefers sunny areas with moist, well-drained soil, such as along creeks, in valleys and ravines, and on upland plains; it tolerates moderate shade but will produce more fruits in areas with ample sun. It grows from the plains to the lower montane zone. A very adaptable plant, it survives occasional drought as well as seasonal flooding.

GROWTH: This stiff-branched, full shrub is generally 3 to 6 feet tall, although it can grow taller in good conditions. Branches are sturdy and reddish-brown; older bark is dark gray to reddish-gray with numerous pale, bumpy lenticels (breathing pores). Golden currant branches have no thorns. Very early spring-blooming yellow flowers with a spicy, clove-like odor give the plant another of its common names, clove currant.

LEAVES: Smooth, flat, thick three-lobed leaves grow alternately on long petioles (stemlets). Leaves are 1 to 2 inches long and wide; the veins fan out from the base where the leaf joins the petiole. The lobes are deeply divided, and each has several large, rounded teeth at the tip.

FRUIT: Round, glossy berries, about ⅓ inch across, grow in racemes (long clusters of multiple fruits; racemes of golden currant may be fairly short) from leaf axils. Ripe berries are generally black to purplish-black, although some reddish or yellow berries may be sweet and soft enough to eat. Stripes, which may be fairly subtle on fully ripe fruits, run longitudinally on the berry; a prominent flower remnant, often called a pigtail, is present at the end of the berry. Although they contain numerous small seeds, the berries are delicious and can be eaten raw or used in baked goods, savory sauces, jams and other dishes. There are no toxic look-alikes.

SEASON: Berries are ripe from mid to late summer.

COMPARE: Several other currants with black fruits grow in our area, but the plants are smaller, with smaller fruits; see pgs. 256, 278, 280. Some gooseberries have similar fruits, but gooseberries have thorns, and their fruits do not grow in racemes; see pgs. 44, 172, 264, 266 and 268.

NOTES: Hummingbirds, butterflies and bees are attracted to the flowers.

green = key identification feature

LARGE
WOODY SHRUB

ALTERNATE
LEAVES

MID TO
LATE SUMMER

Trumpet Gooseberry

Ribes leptanthum

HABITAT: This native gooseberry grows in sunny, well-drained locations from the foothills through the lower sub-alpine zones. It is often found in canyons, along streams and on exposed hillsides.

GROWTH: Trumpet gooseberry is generally 2 to 4 feet in height and has multiple, erect stems; leaves are small, so the plant often looks somewhat open. Leaf nodes have one sharp, tapering thorn up to ½ inch long, which is sometimes flanked by two smaller thorns. Stems are light gray to brownish and are sometimes bristly between the leaf nodes.

LEAVES: Smooth leaves with fine hairs on the edges grow alternately, singly or in small clusters on long, downy petioles (stemlets). Leaves are less than ¾ inch long and generally have five lobes (sometimes three); lobes are deeply scalloped, giving the leaf a frilly appearance. The middle lobe is deeply tapered and narrow at its base where it joins the other lobes.

FRUIT: The smooth, ¼- to ⅓-inch round berry grows on a thin stemlet from leaf nodes, singly or in small clusters. Stripes, which may be fairly subtle on fully ripe fruits, run longitudinally on the berry; a prominent flower remnant, often called a pigtail, is present at the end of the berry. Trumpet gooseberries are green when young, maturing to black or reddish-black when ripe. Gooseberries are edible in both the green and ripe stages; there are no toxic look-alikes.

SEASON: Tubular white flowers that are densely hairy appear in spring; fruits follow, ripening from mid to late summer.

COMPARE: Whitestem gooseberry (pg. 268) has shorter thorns and much larger leaves. Canadian gooseberry (pg. 266) also has shorter thorns and much larger leaves; its stems are bristly. Snow gooseberry (*R. niveum*) has bristly, brownish stems and bluish-black fruits; in our area, it is found in a few Idaho counties. Currants (pgs. 142, 166, 232, 256, 262, 278, 280) look similar but have no thorns; fruits grow in hanging clusters.

NOTES: Ripe gooseberries are excellent in baked desserts. Green gooseberries (pg. 44) are rich in pectin, and are used primarily for jam and jelly.

green = key identification feature

LARGE
WOODY SHRUB

ALTERNATE
LEAVES

MID TO
LATE SUMMER

Canadian Gooseberry

Ribes oxyacanthoides

HABITAT: Several subspecies of this native plant are found in our area, at elevations ranging from the plains to the alpine zones. All look very similar when fruiting; distinguishing between them is difficult, and best left to botanists. Canadian gooseberries are found on rocky sites and sandy shorelines, in canyons and ravines, along streams and in open forests; they require adequate moisture and produce more fruits in areas with ample sun.

GROWTH: An arching shrub, up to 5 feet high, although some subspecies are much shorter. Mature stems are covered with thin bristles, especially on the lower portions of the branches; young stems are finely hairy. Leaf nodes have one to three sharp thorns that are ¼ to ½ inch long.

LEAVES: Attached alternately to the stem by a long petiole (stemlet); each leaf node has one to three leaves. Each leaf has three to five distinct lobes, resembling a maple leaf with rounded teeth. Leaves are up to 1½ inches long. The upper surfaces are dark green with scattered hairs; lower surfaces are paler and more hairy.

FRUIT: The smooth, ⅓- to ½-inch round berry grows on a thin stemlet from leaf nodes, singly or in small clusters. Stripes, which may be fairly subtle on fully ripe fruits, run longitudinally on the berry; a prominent flower remnant, often called a pigtail, is present at the end of the berry. Canadian gooseberries are green when young, maturing to purplish-black to bluish-black when ripe. Gooseberries are edible in both the green and ripe stages; there are no toxic look-alikes.

SEASON: Fruits ripen from mid to late summer.

COMPARE: Please see the text on pgs. 264 for comparisons between various gooseberry species. Currants (pgs. 142, 166, 232, 256, 262, 278, 280) look similar but have no thorns; fruits grow in hanging clusters.

NOTES: Canadian gooseberries occasionally root where the tips touch the ground, creating dense, bristly thickets.

green = key identification feature

LARGE
WOODY SHRUB

ALTERNATE
LEAVES

MID TO
LATE SUMMER

Whitestem Gooseberry

Ribes inerme

HABITAT: This native shrub prefers moist areas. It grows in mixed-wood and pinyon-juniper forests, along streams, on ridges, and at the edges of meadows. Most common in the foothills through the montane zone.

GROWTH: A woody shrub which sometimes grows as a thicket. Stems are 3 to 6 feet long but may arch downward, making the plant appear shorter. Most leaf nodes have one to three stout thorns up to ⅓ inch long. Young stems are tan with fine bristles. Older stems are whitish or gray; they are typically **smooth between leaf nodes** but may have a few thin prickles. Bark on older stems often has **vertical splits or ridges**.

LEAVES: Alternate, up to 1½ inches long, growing singly or in small clusters on very long petioles (stemlets). Each leaf typically has three **fairly deep lobes** with rounded teeth; some leaves have five lobes. Surfaces are smooth or may have fine, downy hairs, especially on the veins.

FRUIT: Smooth rounded berries, up to ⅓ inch across, grow on thin stemlets from leaf nodes, **singly or in small clusters**. Fruits are green when young (see photo, pg. 44), ripening to black or purplish-red; lighter-colored fruits have subtle longitudinal stripes. A prominent flower remnant, often called a pigtail, is attached to the base. Gooseberries are edible in both the green and ripe stages; there are no toxic look-alikes.

SEASON: Ripe fruits are present from mid to late summer.

COMPARE: Desert gooseberry (*R. velutinum*) is similar, but its stems are more brownish and its leaf lobes are shallower; the leaves are leathery, hairy and rough-textured, with small white bumps. In our area, it is found in central and southwestern Idaho, and much of western Utah. Several other gooseberries in our area have blackish fruits; see pgs. 264 and 266. Currants (pgs. 142, 166, 232, 256, 262, 278, 280) look similar but have no thorns; fruits grow in hanging clusters.

NOTES: Ripe gooseberries are excellent in baked desserts; whitestem gooseberries may be sweet enough to enjoy raw when fully ripe.

green = key identification feature

LARGE
WOODY SHRUB

ALTERNATE
LEAVES

MID TO
LATE SUMMER

Black Chokecherry

Prunus virginiana var. *melanocarpa*

HABITAT: Moist, well-drained areas such as mixed-wood or hardwood forests, clearings, parklands, thickets, slopes and alongside rivers and creeks. It grows from the plains through the montane zones.

GROWTH: A large native shrub, up to 15 feet in height but usually much shorter. Generally open in form and somewhat straggly. Bark is reddish-brown to gray and is smooth, with visible lenticels (breathing pores); smaller stems are often reddish. Shrubs frequently form thickets.

LEAVES: Broadly oval, smooth leaves grow alternately on ½ to 1-inch petioles (stemlets) that are often reddish. Leaves are dark green above, paler underneath; edges are finely toothed. Leaves are 2 to 4 inches long, roughly one-half as wide, tapering at or above the middle of the leaf to a broad point. The petiole has several small glands (visible with a lens).

FRUIT: Shiny round drupes, ⅜ inch across, grow in racemes (long clusters of multiple fruits). Ripe fruits are black or purplish-black; they are soft and somewhat translucent. Each drupe contains a single egg-shaped pit which is fairly large in proportion to the amount of flesh. Chokecherries have a delicious sweet-tart flavor, although they may be too tart for many people to enjoy raw. There are no toxic look-alikes.

SEASON: Chokecherries ripen in mid to late summer.

COMPARE: Pin cherries (pg. 188) have narrower leaves; fruits are bright red when ripe and grow in small clusters, each on its own stem, rather than in racemes. Serviceberries (pg. 216) have similar leaves, but the fruit is a pome, an apple-like fruit with a crown on the base. Common chokecherry, *P. virginiana* var. *virginiana*, has fruits that are dark red to reddish-black when ripe; it is found in the eastern half of the U.S. but does not grow in our area.

NOTES: Chokecherry leaves and pits contain hydrocyanic acid, a cyanide-producing compound. The leaves and pits should never be eaten, and care should be taken to avoid crushing chokecherry pits when juicing the fruits. Cooking or drying eliminates the harmful compound.

green = key identification feature

Chokecherry bark

LARGE
WOODY SHRUB

ALTERNATE
LEAVES

MID TO
LATE SUMMER

Western Sand Cherry

Prunus pumila var. besseyi

HABITAT: Open, rocky or sandy areas, including lake and river shorelines, edges of coniferous forests, rocky slopes and grassy prairie areas. Sand cherry prefers sunny areas and tolerates dry conditions; it can survive harsh winters. It grows in the plains and foothills zones.

GROWTH: A sparse, low native shrub, 2 to 9 feet in height, with upright branches. In windy areas, it may recline rather than stand upright. Twigs are reddish; branches are reddish-brown, becoming gray with age. Bark is marked with light-colored lenticels (breathing pores).

LEAVES: Narrowly oval, tapering on both ends, with a leathery texture; they grow alternately from the stems on petioles (stemlets) that are often reddish. Leaves are 1 to 2 inches long and roughly one-third as wide; edges have scattered small teeth, especially toward the tip. Deep green and glossy on top, lighter beneath; tips and leaf edges sometimes have a reddish tinge.

FRUIT: An oval drupe with a single pit; the fruit is about 1 inch long and glossy black when ripe. There is more flesh in proportion to the pit than on chokecherries (pg. 270) or pin cherries (pg. 188). Fruits are edible; they are sweet but somewhat astringent. They are usually cooked to make jam or preserves. There are no toxic look-alikes.

SEASON: Fruits ripen from mid to late summer.

COMPARE: American wild plum (pg. 186) has similar-sized fruits, but they are red when ripe.

NOTES: The deep roots of sand cherry help stabilize sandy areas. The fruit is eaten by large birds; twigs are browsed by deer and small mammals. Birds use the shrubs for nesting and escape cover. Sand cherry leaves, stems and pits contain hydrocyanic acid, a cyanide-producing compound. The leaves and pits should never be eaten, and care should be taken to avoid crushing the pits when juicing the fruits. Cooking or drying eliminates the harmful compound.

green = key identification feature

LARGE
WOODY SHRUB

OPPOSITE
COMPOUND
LEAVES

MID TO
LATE SUMMER

Rocky Mountain Elderberry

Sambucus racemosa var. *melanocarpa*

HABITAT: This native shrub is found in cool, moist locations, such as ditches, streambanks and forest edges; it prefers dappled sun. It grows from the foothills through the montane zones.

GROWTH: A large, fast-growing native shrub; up to 13 feet in height, but typically found much shorter. Bark of older stems is dark reddish-brown and covered with numerous warty lenticels (breathing pores). Younger stems are soft and pithy, and often covered with downy hairs.

LEAVES: Compound leaves, each with five to seven leaflets, grow oppositely on the stem; leaves are 3 to 6 inches long. Leaflets are 2 to 5 inches long, one-third to one-quarter as wide, and oval with a slightly angled or asymmetrical base and pointed tip; edges have fine, sharp teeth. Top sides are medium green and smooth, undersides are paler and downy.

FRUIT: Round drupes, about ⅛ inch across, with two seeds, grow profusely in rounded clusters atop stalks that rise from the leaf axils; fruits are black to purplish-black when ripe, giving the species its other common name, black elderberry. The fruits are rank in flavor and somewhat toxic, especially when raw; cooking may render the fruit—but not the seeds—edible, but opinions vary. Leaves, stems and all other parts of all elderberry species are toxic.

SEASON: Rocky Mountain elderberry flowers in spring, while the leaves are still unfolding. Fruits ripen from mid to late summer, depending on altitude and specific conditions.

COMPARE: Red elderberry (pg. 154) is very similar, but ripe fruits are bright red. Common elderberry (pg. 212) has similar growth habits, but its fruits grow in flat-topped clusters rather than the rounded clusters of Rocky Mountain elderberry; common elderberry leaves have five to 11 leaflets. Fruits of common elderberry are edible when cooked.

NOTES: Some sources list this plant as *S. melanocarpa*.

green = key identification feature

LARGE
WOODY SHRUB

ALTERNATE
LEAVES

LATE
SUMMER

DELICIOUS

Mountain Huckleberry

Vaccinium membranaceum

HABITAT: This native shrub is often the dominant understory plant in moist conifer forests; it is also found in burned-over areas, on rocky hillsides and on talus slopes (an area of broken rock at the base of a cliff). It grows from the foothills through the sub-alpine zones.

GROWTH: This multi-branched shrub is typically 3 to 4 feet tall but may grow up to 6 feet in good conditions. Young branches are yellowish-green or reddish and may be rounded or slightly angled; older stems have shreddy gray bark. Mountain huckleberry spreads by rhizomes (underground root-bearing stems) and often grows in large colonies.

LEAVES: Alternate, oval leaves taper on both ends; edges have very fine teeth all around, and the tip is a slightly rounded point. Leaves are ¾ to 2 inches long and one-half as wide; they have a very short petiole (stemlet) and may appear to be attached directly to the stem. The upper surface is bright green and glossy; undersides are paler and slightly waxy. This plant is also called thinleaf huckleberry because the leaves are very thin.

FRUIT: Round berries with a prominent depression or star-shaped crown on the bottom; when ripe, they are blackish or purplish-black with a very slight bloom. Berries are ¼ to ½ inch across and slightly flattened; they grow singly on short stalks from leaf axils. Ripe berries are delicious raw or cooked, with a sweet-tart flavor. There are no toxic look-alikes.

SEASON: Berries ripen in late summer; leaves turn red or purple in fall.

COMPARE: Oval-leaf blueberry (*V. ovalifolium*) is a related plant with similar appearance, but its leaves are dull with untoothed edges and a more rounded tip, and its ripe fruits are blue with a dusty bloom; in our area, it is found in northern Idaho and scattered locations in Montana. Bilberries (pg. 230) are related plants that are much shorter; ripe fruits are blue.

NOTES: Mountain huckleberry is often considered the best of the blueberry-like fruits that grow in the Rockies, and is the official state fruit of Idaho. The fruits are harvested from the wild for use in jams and other products that are sold throughout the upper Rockies and the Pacific Northwest.

green = key identification feature

LARGE
WOODY SHRUB

ALTERNATE
LEAVES

LATE
SUMMER

Sticky Currant

Ribes viscosissimum

HABITAT: This native shrub prefers moist habitats, and is found on both open and forested slopes, along streams, in shaded woods and canyon bottoms, and on disturbed sites such as clearcuts and burned areas. It grows from the foothills through the lower sub-alpine zones.

GROWTH: An upright shrub up to 6 feet high; some branches may spread out horizontally, giving the shrub a straggly appearance. Young stems are pinkish, tan or gray and covered with fine, sticky hairs; older branches are reddish-brown and hairless, often with shreddy bark. Sticky currant has no prickles or thorns. All parts of the shrub are pleasantly fragrant.

LEAVES: Broad, sticky leaves, up to 3½ inches across and slightly shorter, grow alternately on thick, hairy petioles (stemlets) that are shorter than the leaves. Both surfaces are rough to the touch and covered with tiny, bump-like glands that secrete a sticky fluid. Leaves have a heart-shaped base and three to five fairly shallow lobes with coarse, rounded teeth.

FRUIT: Rounded, slightly oblong berries up to ½ inch long grow in racemes (long clusters of multiple fruits) from leaf axils; a prominent flower remnant, often called a pigtail, is present at the end of the berry. Ripe berries are dull black; they have a gummy, waxy coating and numerous small glands that secrete a sticky fluid. They are edible, although some foragers consider them gummy and distasteful; they may cause intestinal problems in some people. There are no toxic look-alikes.

SEASON: Fruits are ripe in late summer.

COMPARE: Wax currant (pg. 166) has similar leaves, but they are smaller and not as sticky; ripe fruit is red. Redflower currant (*R. sanguineum*) has similar leaves and glandular, bluish to bluish-black fruit with a dusty bloom, but the leaves are much smaller and are not sticky; in our area, it is found only in Idaho, primarily in a few northern counties.

NOTES: Sticky currant was collected in Idaho in June, 1806, by members of the Lewis and Clark expedition; prior to this, the species was apparently undocumented by biologists.

green = key identification feature

LARGE
WOODY SHRUB

ALTERNATE
LEAVES

LATE
SUMMER

Prickly Currant

Ribes lacustre

HABITAT: Also known as swamp currant, this native shrub prefers moist areas, and is found in wetlands and along lakes and streams; it will tolerate drier areas that are partially shaded, and is also found on forested slopes and in canyons. It grows from the plains to the sub-alpine zone.

GROWTH: Prickly currant stems are up to 5 feet long; according to data from the U.S. Forest Service, the stems are erect when the plant is growing in sunlight, but in shade, they recline, making the plant appear much shorter. Stems are reddish to brownish and **very bristly or prickly**, giving rise to another common name, bristly black currant. Leaf nodes have **five or more thin, sharp spines that are ¼ inch long or shorter.**

LEAVES: Alternate, growing singly or in small clusters on very long, lightly bristly petioles (stemlets). Leaves are **1 to 2 inches long and wide**; both surfaces are **smooth and lustrous** with a few scattered hairs, especially on the veins. Each leaf has three to five lobes with rounded teeth; the middle lobe is deeply tapered at its base where it joins the other lobes.

FRUIT: Round berries, ¼ to ⅓ inch across, grow in racemes (long clusters of multiple fruits) from leaf axils; the berries are covered with **short hairs that have rounded glands at the tips** (visible with a lens). A short flower remnant is present at the end of the berry. Berries are green when first formed, turning red before ripening to black or purplish black. They are edible; some foragers consider them delicious, while others find the hairy surface unappealing. Eating quality varies from plant to plant, and may also vary depending on habitat. There are no toxic look-alikes.

SEASON: Saucer-shaped pink or purple flowers appear in early summer. Fruits follow, and are ripe in late summer.

COMPARE: Several other currants with black fruits grow in our area; please see pgs. 256, 262 and 278 for descriptions. Gooseberry currant (pg. 172) has bristly stems with one to three short spines at the leaf nodes, but its leaves are hairy and less than ¾ inch long; ripe fruits are red.

NOTES: Some people have an allergic reaction after touching the bristles.

green = key identification feature

Prickly stem

NOT EDIBLE

LARGE
WOODY SHRUB

ALTERNATE
LEAVES (TYP.)

LATE
SUMMER

Smith's Buckthorn

Rhamnus smithii

HABITAT: This native shrub grows in sunny, well-drained areas, such as open woodlands, grassy hillsides, meadows and valleys; it is often found in rocky areas. It is an uncommon plant that grows in the foothills zone.

GROWTH: A somewhat open deciduous shrub, usually 6 to 10 feet tall and wide. Multiple stems grow from the base; they may reach upright or may arch and bend to the sides. Twigs are downy, becoming smooth with age. Branches are gray to brownish-gray, and often somewhat knobby; along the lower portions of the branches, spur branches grow outward in a perpendicular fashion. Smith's buckthorn has no thorns or spines.

LEAVES: Glossy, narrowly oval leaves, 1 to 2¼ inches long and one-third as wide, grow on short, pale petioles (stemlets). They grow alternately or, sometimes, nearly oppositely, often in small clusters (particularly at branch tips). Leaf tips are softly pointed; bases are tapered. Edges have fine teeth all around. The numerous side veins are fairly straight to slightly curving; the veins and midrib are yellowish and prominent on the undersides. Leaves are smooth and hairless on both sides.

FRUIT: Rounded berry-like drupes, about ⅓ inch across, grow on short stemlets along the branches. Ripe fruits are opaque black; the surface is smooth but not particularly glossy. Edibility information is not available, but this plant belongs to a family whose fruits are generally considered inedible or toxic; it is best to consider the fruits inedible.

SEASON: Fruits are ripe in late summer.

COMPARE: Sawleaf buckthorn (*R. serrata*; also listed as *R. fasciculata*) is a related plant, but it is up to 15 feet tall and its leaves are hairy underneath; in our area, it is found only in the central counties of the southern half of New Mexico. Stretchberry (pg. 210) has a similar overall appearance, but its ripe fruits are purplish with a light bloom. Cascara buckthorn (pg. 294) has similar leaves and fruits, but it is taller; it grows in the northern part of our area, while Smith's buckthorn grows only in the southern part.

NOTES: Smith's buckthorn grows only in Colorado and New Mexico.

green = key identification feature

EDIBLE

LARGE
WOODY SHRUB

ALTERNATE
LEAVES

SUMMER
THROUGH FALL

Warnock's Snakewood

Condalia warnockii

HABITAT: This thorny native grows in sandy or gravelly desert habitat, including washes, drainages, canyons and slopes. It is found in the plains zone, particularly in semi-desert shrublands.

GROWTH: A multi-branched shrub that is typically 4 to 6 feet tall, with nearly equal spread at the top. The main trunk branches are stout and twisted, with gray to grayish-brown bark; secondary branches may arch or grow upright, and have gray to tan bark. Short spine-tipped branches grow at right angles to the secondary branches. Tiny, pleasantly fragrant yellow flowers grow along the branches from leaf clusters. When leaves are present, snakewood can look very full; when the leaves have dropped, it often looks skeletal and distorted.

LEAVES: Tiny, elliptic to paddle-shaped leaves, ⅛ to ⅜ inch long, grow alternately or in small clusters along the branches. Leaves are dull greenish-gray above, paler below; they are thick and covered with fine hairs, and the underside has deeply depressed veins that make the leaf look wrinkled.

FRUIT: Rounded drupes, slightly less than ¼ inch long with a large stone, grow singly on short stemlets from leaf clusters. Fruits are green when young, turning red, then purplish, before maturing to glossy black. Ripe fruits are edible; quality varies, and they may be sweet or slightly bitter.

SEASON: Warnock's snakewood flowers twice: once in early spring, and a second time during the desert's rainy season in mid to late summer. Fruits ripen from summer through fall.

COMPARE: Javelina bush (pg. 148) is a thorny, multi-branched shrub, but it is a shorter shrub with strap-shaped leaves and football-shaped fruits that are red when ripe. Lotebush (pg. 242) is a tall thorny shrub with waxy-looking branches and larger leaves; its fruits are blue when ripe.

NOTES: Birds relish the berries, and also build nests in the thorny plants to get protection from predators. Another common name for this plant is Mexican crucillo.

green = key identification feature

LARGE
WOODY SHRUB

ALTERNATE
COMPOUND
LEAVES

MIDSUMMER
TO FALL

Himalayan Blackberry

Rubus armeniacus

HABITAT: This Eurasian shrub was brought to the United States in the late 1880s for its fruit, and has become naturalized in many areas, especially on the West coast. An adaptable plant, it is not too particular about soil quality, but requires adequate moisture and sun to produce fruits; it is often found on disturbed sites, such as logged areas, waste ground, parking lot borders, field margins and railroad grades. It grows primarily in the plains zone, but may also be found in the foothills.

GROWTH: Himalayan blackberries are brambles, sprawling vine-like shrubs that form thickets. Stems, called canes, grow to 40 feet in length, and are usually arching; they root where they touch the ground. Older canes are ridged, and star-shaped in cross-section; they are purplish-red with numerous sharp, curved thorns.

LEAVES: Compound, doubly toothy, coarsely textured leaves with sharply pointed tips and long stems are attached alternately to the canes; undersides are pale. Leaves of fruiting canes have three leaflets, while those of non-fruiting canes typically have five. Leaflets are 1½ to 3 inches long; the terminal leaflet is often larger than side leaflets.

FRUIT: A compound drupe, ¾ to 1 inch long. Young fruits are green and hard, turning red before ripening to glossy black. The receptacle (core) remains inside the picked berry so the fruit is solid, not hollow like a raspberry. Blackberries are edible raw or cooked; there are no toxic look-alikes.

SEASON: Himalayan blackberries are red and underripe in early summer; they ripen from midsummer to fall, later than native blackberries.

COMPARE: Cutleaf blackberry (*R. laciniatus*) is another non-native blackberry, but its leaves are wrinkly and have very deep, jagged-looking teeth; in our area it is found in about the same locations as Himalayan blackberry. Trailing blackberry (pg. 252) is a native species that is a low-growing, vine-like plant. Whitebark raspberries (pg. 254) and red raspberries (pg. 138) are similar brambles, but picked fruits are hollow.

NOTES: Blackberries have larger, coarser seeds than other brambles.

green = key identification feature

Ridged cane, 5-part leaf

LARGE
WOODY SHRUB

OPPOSITE
LEAVES

LATE SUMMER
TO EARLY FALL

European Privet

Ligustrum vulgare

HABITAT: European privet is an ornamental plant imported from Europe that is frequently used in landscaping; it has escaped into the wild in scattered parts of our area. In cultivation, privets do best in moist, well-drained areas with full sun, but they can grow in shade if the soil is rich. In the wild, they grow in fields, disturbed areas and bottomland forests, as well as along roadsides and forest edges. Escaped plants are most likely to be found in the plains and foothills zones, particularly near cities.

GROWTH: A leafy, multi-branched shrub that may grow to 15 feet in height and width; they spread by suckering and often form dense thickets. Branches are brownish-gray, with numerous lenticels (breathing pores); they tend to be long and arching. The trunk is often hard to see due to all the leaves; it is gray and rough but not fissured.

LEAVES: Glossy, oval to lance-shaped leaves that taper on both ends grow oppositely on short, hairy petioles (stemlets); leaf edges are untoothed. Leaves often grow at almost a right angle to the branch. They are up to 2½ inches long and one-quarter as wide; leaves are smooth and hairless on both surfaces.

FRUIT: Oval to round drupes, ¼ to ⅓ inch long, grow in large clusters at branch tips; they also are scattered in smaller clusters along the branches. Ripe fruits are glossy black to purplish-black. The fruits are considered toxic, reportedly causing intestinal problems.

SEASON: Small white flowers appear in early to midsummer. Fruits follow, ripening from late summer to early fall; they often persist through winter.

COMPARE: Common buckthorn (pg. 292) and other buckthorns have black berries, but leaf edges are toothy and the plants aren't as full as privet.

NOTES: European privet is considered an invasive species due to its aggressive growth, which smothers out native plants.

green = key identification feature

LARGE
WOODY SHRUB

ALTERNATE
LEAVES

LATE SUMMER
TO EARLY FALL

Cotoneaster (several)

Cotoneaster spp.

HABITAT: Cotoneaster is an ornamental plant imported from Asia that is frequently used in landscaping; it has escaped into the wild in scattered parts of our area. In cultivation, cotoneasters do best in moist, well-drained areas with full sun to partial shade. Escaped plants are most likely to be found in the plains and foothills zones, particularly near cities.

GROWTH: Authorities seem to disagree on which species of cotoneaster is found in our area. According to the USDA PLANTS Database, it is Peking cotoneaster (*Cotoneaster acutifolius*); however, the Biota of North American Program lists it as shiny or hedge cotoneaster (*C. lucidus*; also listed as *C. acutifolius* var. *lucidus*). Differences between the two plants are slight. Both are deciduous shrubs, typically 6 to 10 feet tall and equally wide. Bark is medium brown, with bumpy lenticels (breathing pores) and a somewhat scaly texture.

LEAVES: The oval leaves grow alternately on short petioles (stemlets). They are 1 to 2½ inches long and one-half as wide; edges have fine teeth all around, and the tip is pointed. Leaves are deep green on top, paler below; shiny cotoneaster are smooth above and slightly hairy below, while those of Peking cotoneaster are typically hairy on both surfaces.

FRUIT: Oblong pomes, ½ inch across, grow in clusters on long stemlets from branch tips. The fruits have a distinct star-shaped indentation on the base; flesh inside is orangish, and there are two to four hard seeds. The fruits are regarded as inedible; some sources list them as mildly toxic.

SEASON: The fruits ripen throughout summer, turning black in late summer to early fall.

COMPARE: Hawthorns (pg. 192) resemble ripening cotoneaster, but hawthorn leaves are longer, with larger, coarser teeth; fruits have a crown-shaped floral remnant that projects from the base and the flesh is whitish rather than orangish.

NOTES: Cotoneaster may be somewhat uncommon in the wild at the present time, but its range is likely to increase as birds spread the seeds.

green = key identification feature

Ripening fruit

Ripe fruit

Smashed fruit

LARGE
WOODY SHRUB

OPPOSITE
LEAVES

LATE SUMMER
TO EARLY FALL

Common Buckthorn

Rhamnus cathartica

HABITAT: Open hardwood forests, prairie areas, fields, forest edges, urban parks, shelterbelts, floodplains, ravines and fencerows. Prefers partial shade but can tolerate moist or dry conditions. Specific elevation information is not available, but common buckthorn is most likely to be found in the plains and foothills zones.

GROWTH: A large, multi-stemmed shrub with a spreading crown; up to 20 feet in height but usually much shorter. Bark is gray to brown; older stems are roughly textured, with long, corky protrusions. Twigs often have a spine at the tip, giving the species its common name.

LEAVES: Dark, glossy green, broadly oval leaves with a pointed tip and a broad base grow oppositely on long petioles (stemlets). Leaves are 1½ to 3 inches long, and roughly two-thirds as wide; both surfaces are hairless. Edges are finely toothy; each leaf has three to five pairs of deep veins that curve in toward the tip to follow the edge of the leaf. Leaves remain green into fall, long after most shrubs have lost their leaves.

FRUIT: Glossy, round black drupes, about ¼ inch in diameter, grow on thin stemlets in dense clusters at leaf axils, or singly along the stems. The fruits are strongly cathartic, and are considered toxic.

SEASON: Common buckthorn ripens in late summer to early fall.

COMPARE: Several other plants with black fruits may be confused with common buckthorn; none have a spine at the tip. European privet (pg. 288) has long, narrow leaves with smooth edges. Glossy buckthorn and Cascara buckthorn (pg. 294) have smooth-edged leaves that are typically alternate; leaf undersides are hairy. Smith's buckthorn (pg. 282) has long, narrow leaves with much shorter petioles.

NOTES: Common buckthorn is a non-native species, imported in the late 1800s from Europe for use as a landscape plant. It has naturalized, and is considered invasive throughout most of its range. It spreads rapidly, crowding out native plants.

green = key identification feature

LARGE SHRUB
OR SMALL TREE

ALTERNATE
LEAVES (TYP.)

SUMMER

*see below

Cascara Buckthorn –AND–
Glossy Buckthorn

Frangula spp.

HABITAT: These two related plants grow in the plains zone, in moist areas, including open woods, canyons, wetlands, streambanks and pond edges.

GROWTH: Cascara buckthorn (*Frangula purshiana*; also listed as *Rhamnus purshiana*) is a native multi-stemmed shrub or tree up to 35 feet tall. Glossy buckthorn (*F. alnus*; also listed as *R. frangula*) is 20 feet or less; it is a non-native plant that was brought to the U.S. in the 1800s as an ornamental. Twigs of both are reddish-brown with fine hairs; larger branches are grayish-brown. Cascara buckthorn often has patches of white lichen on the bark, while glossy buckthorn has noticeable, bumpy lenticels (breathing pores). The inner bark of Cascara buckthorn is yellow.

LEAVES: Alternate, but some glossy buckthorn leaves may grow oppositely. Cascara buckthorn leaves are up to 6 inches long and one-third as wide; edges have very fine, scalloped teeth. Glossy buckthorn leaves are 2 to 4 inches long and one-half as wide; edges are smooth. Leaves of both are deep green above, lighter below, with deep veins that form a V at the midrib, then curve near the edges to follow the contour of the leaf.

FRUIT: Round, glossy drupes grow on short stemlets from the leaf axils; glossy buckthorn fruits are about ¼ inch across, while Cascara's may be up to ½ inch. Fruits are green at first, turning red before ripening to black. They are mildly toxic and inedible; Cascara's fruits have laxative qualities.

SEASON: Fruits are on the plant from early through late summer. Green, red and black fruits may all be present on the plant at the same time.

COMPARE: Common buckthorn (pg. 292) has opposite, toothy leaves that are more rounded.

NOTES: At the time of this writing, glossy buckthorn has been found only in a few counties in Colorado, Idaho and Wyoming; however, it has demonstrated aggressive, invasive tendencies in other states and its range in our area is likely to increase.

green = key identification feature   *combined range

Glossy buckthorn

LARGE SHRUB
OR SMALL TREE

ALTERNATE
LEAVES

SUMMER
THROUGH FALL

Allthorn –or– Crown of Thorns *Koeberlinia spinosa*

HABITAT: A native shrub or small tree that grows in a band along both sides of the Mexican border, allthorn is found in dry, open areas, such as hillsides, mesa tops, plains and scrublands. It requires full sun and tolerates drought, and grows in desert areas of the plains zone.

GROWTH: A densely branched shrub that is typically 2 to 10 feet tall and equally wide; occasionally, a plant develops a large, woody central trunk and grows as a tree up to 20 feet tall. Older branches are gray with a rough, scaly texture. The majority of the plant is composed of stiff greenish branches, each with numerous **short, round greenish branchlets that grow at right angles** to the branch. The branchlets taper into **sharp, black- or brown-tipped thorns,** and also have additional short thorn-tipped branchlets growing at right angles along their length. Overall, the plant looks like a **greenish mass of crisscrossing thorns.** From spring through fall, tiny white flowers bloom in clusters along the branchlets after a rain; flowering is most common during the rainy season in fall.

LEAVES: Allthorn is leafless most of the year; photosynthesis is handled by the greenish branchlets. In spring after a rain, tiny oval leaves less than ¼ inch long grow alternately along the branchlets; however, they fall off almost immediately and the plant remains leafless until the next rain.

FRUIT: Round berries less than ¼ inch across grow on thin stalks in dense clusters along the branchlets. Berries are yellowish-green when immature, turning various shades of pink, orangish, maroon and purple before ripening to black. Clusters may have berries of many colors at the same time. According to information from the University of Arizona, American Indians apparently ate the fruits; modern accounts of edibility or preparation are lacking, so it may be best to consider the fruits inedible.

SEASON: Ripe fruits are present from early summer through late fall.

COMPARE: Nothing in our area looks like allthorn. Crucifixion thorn (*Castela emoryi*) is similar, but it grows only in southern Arizona and California.

NOTES: The wood is oily and produces black smoke when burned.

green = key identification feature

Immature fruits

Ripe fruits

LARGE SHRUB
OR SMALL TREE

OPPOSITE
LEAVES

LATE SUMMER
TO EARLY FALL

Nannyberry

Viburnum lentago

HABITAT: Openings and edges in moist, well-drained hardwood and mixed-wood forests; also found along roadsides and streambanks. It is found primarily in the plains zone, but can also grow in the foothills.

GROWTH: An open, multi-stemmed small native tree or large shrub, up to 20 feet in height. Often leggy and unkempt-looking. The stems are tan to reddish-brown; tips develop a long, pointed "dragon's claw" in fall.

LEAVES: Smooth, light green leaves grow oppositely, attached to the stems by petioles (stemlets) that have flattened, wavy edges; leaves are oval, 2 to 4 inches long and one-half as wide. Bases are rounded; leaves are widest near the base, tapering to a long point. Leaves are glossy and hairless on both surfaces; edges are finely toothed all around. Leaves turn maroon in fall and may be gone by the time the fruit ripens.

FRUIT: Oval drupes, about ½ inch long with a large, flat pit, grow on reddish stemlets in a loose cluster. The cluster grows directly from the tip of the branch; although individual stemlets may branch to give the appearance of a stalk, close inspection will reveal that there is no intervening stalk between the last pair of leaves and the base of the stemlets. Immature fruits are greenish-white, turning dull red before ripening to bluish-black with a dusty bloom. Ripe fruits are delicious raw or cooked; there are no toxic look-alikes, but the pit is a nuisance.

SEASON: Nannyberries ripen in late summer to early fall, and often persist through winter. Withered nannyberries, if still present on the plant in late fall or winter, make a tasty trail nibble.

COMPARE: Wayfaringtree (*V. lantana*) is a similar, related plant with very wrinkly leaves and edible but bitter fruits; its fruit clusters are denser and larger and ripen more unevenly, and a cluster may have pink, red and blue fruits at the same time. In our area, it is found only in a few counties in Montana, Wyoming and Colorado.

NOTES: A delicious fruit, worth the trouble to remove the pit.

green = key identification feature

Wavy petiole,
dragon's claw

TREE

ALTERNATE
LEAVES

LATE SUMMER
TO EARLY FALL

Common Hackberry

Celtis occidentalis

HABITAT: This native tree is found in rich valleys and bottomlands, hardwood forests, waste ground, fencerows and old fields. It prefers full sun and moist soils, but can adapt to drier areas. It grows in the plains zone.

GROWTH: A tall, full tree, 40 to 60 feet in height with almost equal spread. Lower branches often droop toward the ground. Young stems are tan or reddish, with a zigzag habit; branches are brown, with light-colored lenticels (breathing pores). Bark on the trunk is dark gray and ridged, with an unusual corky, warty texture.

LEAVES: Rough-textured, dull green, alternate leaves are shaped like an elongated heart with a sharply pointed tip; undersides are pale. Leaves are 3 to 5 inches long and one-half as wide; they are widest near the base, which is rounded and often slightly angled. Three of the leaf veins meet at the base of the leaf. Edges have large, pointed teeth except around the base, which has smooth edges. Leaves often develop spots and galls in late summer.

FRUIT: Round drupes, ¼ to ⅓ inch in diameter, grow singly or in pairs on long stemlets from the leaf axils; they are black or blackish-purple when ripe. The flesh is thin in comparison to the size of the pit; however, it is sweet and delicious. There are no toxic look-alikes that grow on trees.

SEASON: Fruits ripen in late summer to early fall, and may persist through winter if not eaten by birds and squirrels.

COMPARE: Netleaf hackberry (pg. 196) is a related but much shorter plant which often grows as a shrub; its ripe fruits are orangish-red to reddish-brown and its leaves have prominent, net-like veins on both sides.

NOTES: Birds eat the berries and nest in the trees; deer browse the leaves and twigs.

green = key identification feature

Hackberry bark

TENDER
PLANT

ALTERNATE
LEAVES

MID TO
LATE SUMMER

Alpine Cancer-Root

Conopholis alpina

HABITAT: Cancer-root does not produce chlorophyll, so it does not require sunlight; it is found under oaks and ponderosa pine in the foothills zone.

GROWTH: Alpine cancer-root is a tender, upright plant that is 6 to 8 inches tall; it typically grows in small colonies. Individual stems are thick, fleshy and unbranched. During the flowering stage, stems are covered with tightly and evenly spaced rows of cream-colored flowers growing from tubular bases; the flowers bend outward from the stem so the plants look like large, elongated whitish pinecones standing upright on the forest floor. Cancer-root produces no chlorophyll; it gets its nutrients from fungi that, in turn, survive by extracting nutrients from trees and other plants (this relationship is called mycoheterotrophy).

LEAVES: Triangular, brownish scale-like leaves, up to ½ inch long and two-thirds as wide, grow alternately, pressed tightly against the stem. Long bracts (leaf-like structures) also grow against the tubular base of the flowers; the bracts are yellowish-white with brown tips.

FRUIT: Rounded white capsules, about ½ inch across, replace the flowers; they are nestled in the dried brown remnants of the floral tube. The capsules have fairly thick skins and are filled with a large number of small yellowish seeds; eventually, the capsules dry out, splitting to release their seeds. The fruits are not edible.

SEASON: Alpine cancer-root flowers from mid-spring to early summer; the fruits develop in mid to late summer.

COMPARE: American cancer-root (*C. americana*) is very similar in appearance, but it is found only east of the Mississippi River.

NOTES: This plant is also called by the racially offensive name of alpine squawroot; ground cone is another common name. Many sources list this plant as *Conopholis alpina* var. *mexicana*; since there are no other subspecies of *Conopholis alpina*, the full name is often not used.

green = key identification feature

Fruits

SMALL
WOODY SHRUB

ALTERNATE
COMPOUND
LEAVES

LATE SUMMER
THROUGH FALL

Western Poison Ivy

Toxicodendron rydbergii

HABITAT: This native plant is found in moist areas with moderate sun, such as canyons, road ditches, open woodlands, fencelines, swampy areas and streambanks; also found in agricultural fields, sandy areas and disturbed sites. It grows from the plains through the montane zones and is also found in semi-desert shrublands.

GROWTH: Western poison ivy grows as a shrub that is typically 1 to 3 feet high, but can grow to 6 feet tall; it may also appear as a short, tender leafy plant. Patches of poison ivy may be dense and extensive. Poison ivy has the classic three-part leaf configuration leading to the old saying, "Leaves of three, let it be."

LEAVES: Three-part leaves grow on the ends of long stalks attached alternately to the stem. Leaflets are smooth and glossy green, with irregular toothy or wavy edges; the petiole (stemlet) of the middle leaflet is longer than those of the side leaflets. Leaflets are 2 to 4 inches long; they turn red in fall.

FRUIT: The round, ridged berries, ⅛ to ³⁄₁₆ inch across, are greenish when immature, ripening to white or yellowish. They grow in upright clusters near the main stem. All parts the plant are toxic and may cause a painful rash if touched; smoke from burning poison ivy can cause a severe allergic reaction.

SEASON: Berries develop in summer, ripening from late summer through fall, and may persist into winter.

COMPARE: Members of the *Rubus* genus including raspberries (pgs. 136, 138, 140) and blackberries (pgs. 252, 286) have toothy 3-part leaflets, but they are brambles (vine-like shrubs) with thorny or bristly stems; their fruits are compound drupes.

NOTES: The toxic compound in poison ivy, urushiol, remains active, even in the winter, on everything it touches, until washed off. Many people have no reaction to the compound until repeated exposure; never assume you are immune to the effects because sensitivity could develop at any time.

green = key identification feature

LARGE
WOODY SHRUB

OPPOSITE
LEAVES

MID TO
LATE SUMMER

Red-Osier Dogwood

Cornus sericea

HABITAT: This native shrub prefers slightly damp soil and is found in open woodlands, along streams and in swampy areas. It grows from the plains through the montane zones.

GROWTH: A bushy shrub, typically 4 to 6 feet in height but sometimes much larger; it often grows as a spreading thicket. Young stems are reddish, purplish or green splotched with red; they turn bright, deep red in fall. Older stems are light brown with numerous lenticels (breathing pores); young stems have fine hairs.

LEAVES: Egg-shaped to narrowly oval leaves, 1 to 4 inches long and about one-half as wide, grow oppositely on ½-inch petioles (stemlets) that are often reddish; tips are sharply pointed and bases are roundly tapered. Leaves have smooth edges; the top sides are medium green and smooth, while the undersides are silvery-green with fine hairs. Distinct veins curve in towards the pointy tip. Leaves turn purplish in fall.

FRUIT: White, round drupes, ¼ inch across, have a small protrusion on the bottom; some fruits may be tinged with blue. The fruits are in a cluster at the end of a stalk that grows from a leaf axil or branch tip. Red-osier dogwood fruits are bitter and are generally regarded as inedible; however, American Indians ate them occasionally, often mixed with sweeter fruits.

SEASON: Fruits mature from mid to late summer.

COMPARE: Snowberry (pg. 308) have white fruits, but the leaves are more rounded and the plants are generally smaller.

NOTES: Dogwood fruits are eaten by many birds, including cardinals, woodpeckers, wood ducks and upland birds; deer browse on the fruits, leaves and twigs. Dogwood is a host to the spring azure butterfly. Some texts list this plant as *C. alba* or *C. stolonifera*; others refer to it as *Swida sericea*.

green = key identification feature

NOT EDIBLE

LARGE WOODY SHRUB OPPOSITE LEAVES LATE SUMMER

Mountain Common Western Round-leaf

Snowberries (several)

Symphoricarpos spp.

HABITAT: Four native snowberries are common in various parts of our area. Mountain snowberry (*Symphoricarpos oreophilus*) and common snowberry (*S. albus*) are adaptable and grow in moist, well-drained areas as well as fairly dry, rocky areas. Western snowberry (*S. occidentalis*) prefers moist areas like ravines, floodplains, lakeshores and streambanks. Roundleaf snowberry (*S. rotundifolius*) grows in open forests and in rocky canyons. Common and western snowberry grow from the plains through the montane zones; mountain snowberry, from foothills to sub-alpine zones, and roundleaf snowberry in the montane and sub-alpine zones.

GROWTH: Erect, stiff-branched shrubs, generally 2 to 5 feet tall; plants in rich soil with adequate moisture may be taller. Snowberries spread by rhizomes (underground root-bearing stems) and often form dense colonies.

LEAVES: Oval to egg-shaped leaves grow oppositely on short petioles (stemlets); edges may have several large, irregular lobes or teeth. Leaves of western snowberry are up to 3½ inches long. Common snowberry's leaves are 2 inches long or shorter; mountain snowberry's are up to 1¼ inches long. Roundleaf snowberry leaves are less than ¾ inch long.

FRUIT: Rounded whitish, waxy drupes up to ½ inch across with a flower remnant on the end grow singly or in clusters from leaf axils and on branch tips; they are sometimes lumpy. Fruits of all four are inedible; most sources list them as toxic when eaten in quantity.

SEASON: Fruits ripen in late summer, and may persist until spring.

COMPARE: A related plant, desert snowberry (*S. longiflorus*) is similar, but its leaves are ½ inch long or less. It is drought-tolerant; in our area, it is found primarily in Utah, in semi-desert shrublands and dry, rocky areas.

NOTES: Flowers may be white or pink; shapes help identify the species. Mountain and roundleaf snowberry flowers are tubular, while common snowberry are more rounded; in all three, the stamens and styles (see pg. 8) are contained within the petals. Western snowberry's flower is broader and more open; the stamens and styles extend beyond the petals.

green = key identification feature

Mountain snowberry

Mountain snowberry flower

Common snowberry flower

Western snowberry flower

LARGE
WOODY SHRUB

ALTERNATE
LEAVES

LATE SUMMER
TO EARLY FALL

Silverberry

Elaeagnus commutata

HABITAT: This native shrub prefers well-drained areas with ample sun; it is found on prairies, in grasslands and cool forests, along streams and near springs. It grows from the plains through the montane zones.

GROWTH: An erect, multi-branched shrub from 3 to 15 feet tall, silverberry grows from spreading underground rhizomes (root-bearing stems) and often forms thickets. Twigs are tan, while older branches are reddish-brown; both are dotted with fine, silvery scales. The shrubs are thornless. Tubular flowers, yellow inside and silvery-yellow outside, grow in small clusters from leaf axils in midsummer; the flowers have a very sweet, lemony scent that can be detected from a long distance.

LEAVES: Narrowly oval leaves with softly pointed tips and smooth edges are silvery-green above, while the undersides are more silvery; both sides are covered with silvery scales and the undersides may have scattered brown scales. Leaves grow alternately on short, broad petioles (stemlets) and are generally 1 to 3 inches long and one-third as wide.

FRUIT: Oval drupes, about ⅜ inch long with a single large stone, are dull white to whitish-tan when ripe and covered with fine silvery scales. Fruits grow singly along the stems from short, scaly stemlets. The fruit, although dry and mealy, is usually sweet, and can be eaten raw, cooked to add to baked goods, or used for jam. It is quite astringent when under-ripe; on individual plants, even ripe fruits may be too astringent to eat.

SEASON: Fruits ripen from late summer to early fall.

COMPARE: Russian olive (pg. 66) is a similar but non-native plant that grows as a tree; its fruits are slightly larger and are yellow when ripe, and its leaves are much narrower.

NOTES: Silverberry is browsed extensively by moose, elk, mule deer and other wildlife. The hard seeds have been used by American Indians as beads or buttons, and were used by the Inuit to decorate garments. Wolf willow is another common name for this plant.

green = key identification feature

HELPFUL RESOURCES AND BIBLIOGRAPHY

Information on wild plants is readily available in books, magazines and on the Internet. Websites from University Extension Services, arboretums, colleges and institutions of higher learning are generally more reliable than personal websites. Here is a list of some websites and books that provide information that may be of interest to readers.

Websites

CactiGuide.com, On-line Guide to the Positive Identification of Members of the Cactus Family, Daiv Freeman. (cactiguide.com)

Early Detection & Distribution Mapping Systems, which shows current, known locations of invasive plants. (eddmaps.org)

Eat the Weeds, Deane Jordan. (eattheweeds.com)

Montana Field Guide. (fieldguide.mt.gov/)

Northern Rockies Natural History Guide, The University of Montana, Missoula. (nhguide.dbs.umt.edu/)

Southwest Colorado Wildflowers, Al Schneider. (swcoloradowildflowers.com)

University of Connecticut Plant Database, Dr. Mark H. Brand. (hort.uconn.edu/Plants/)

Vanderbilt University, Department of Biological Sciences, Nashville, TN 37240. (cas.vanderbilt.edu/bioimages)

Vascular Plants of the Gila Wilderness, Western New Mexico University Department of Natural Sciences and the Dale A. Zimmerman Herbarium, Dr. Russ Kleinman (wnmu.edu/academic/nspages/gilaflora/index.html)

Virginia Tech, College of Natural Resources, Forestry Department, Blacksburg, VA 24061. (cnr.vt.edu/)

Books

Bowers, Nora and Rick, and Stan Tekiela. *Cactus of Arizona*. Cambridge, MN: Adventure Publications, Inc., 2008.

Brill, Steven. *Identifying and Harvesting Edible and Medicinal Plants in Wild (and Not So Wild) Places*. New York: William Morrow, 1994.

Elmore, Francis H. *Shrubs and Trees of the Southwest Uplands*. Tucson, AZ: Western National Parks Association, 1976.

Harrington, H.D. *Edible Native Plants of the Rocky Mountains*. Albuquerque: The University of New Mexico Press, 1967.

Irwin, Pamela and David. *Colorado's Newest and Best Wildflower Hikes* and *Colorado's Best Wildflower Hikes, Volume 3: The San Juan Mountains*. Boulder, CO: Westcliffe Publishers, 2008 and 2006.

Kershaw, Linda, Andy MacKinnon and Jim Pojar. *Plants of the Rocky Mountains*. Auburn, WA: Lone Pine Publishing, 1998.

Marrone, Teresa. *Abundantly Wild: Collecting and Cooking Wild Edibles in the Upper Midwest*. Cambridge, MN: Adventure Publications, Inc., 2004.

Petrides, George A. and Olivia. *A Field Guide to Western Trees*. New York: Houghton Mifflin, 1998 and 1992.

Phillips, H. Wayne. *Plants of the Lewis & Clark Expedition*. Missoula, MT: Mountain Press Publishing Company, 2003.

Seebeck, Cattail Bob. *Best-Tasting Wild Plants of Colorado and the Rockies*. Boulder, CO: Westcliffe Publishers, 1998.

Symonds, George W.D. *The Shrub Identification Book* and *The Tree Identification Book*. New York: Harper Collins, 1963 and 1958.

Thayer, Samuel. *The Forager's Harvest* and *Nature's Garden*. Birchwood, WI: Forager's Harvest, 2006 and 2010.

REFERENCES CONSULTED BY THE AUTHOR

Websites

Amelanchier Systematics and Evolution, Christopher S. Campbell. (sbe.umaine.edu/amelanchier/). Accessed from June 2011 to September 2011.

The Biota of North America Program (BONAP). 2011. North American Plant Atlas, J.T. Kartesz (bonap.org/MapSwitchboard.html). Chapel Hill, N.C. Accessed from January 2011 to November 2011.

Flora of North America. (eFloras.org). Accessed from January 2011 to November 2011.

Southwest Environmental Information Network, SEINet. 2009–2011. (swbiodiversity.org/seinet/index.php). Accessed from January 2011 to November 2011.

U.S. Department of Agriculture, NRCS. 2011. The PLANTS Database National Plant Data Team, Greensboro, NC 27401-4901 USA (plants.usda.gov). Accessed from January 2011 to November 2011.

U.S. Forest Service, Washington, D.C. 20250. (www.fs.fed.us/). Accessed from January 2011 to October 2011.

Books

Dirr, Michael A. *Manual of Woody Landscape Plants*. Champaign, IL: Stipes Publishing, 1998 (fifth edition).

Elpel, Thomas J. *Botany in a Day*. Pony, MT: HOPS Press LLC, 2008.

Smith, Welby R. *Trees and Shrubs of Minnesota*. Minneapolis: University of Minnesota Press, 2008.

Stevens, Russell L. and Coffey, Chuck R. *Trees, Shrubs and Woody Vines: A Pictorial Guide*. Ardmore, OK: The Samuel Roberts Noble Foundation, 2008.

GLOSSARY

Aggregate drupe: A fleshy fruit formed from a single flower but composed of many drupes, each containing one seed; synonymous with compound drupe.

Alpine zone: The area above the treeline, generally above 10,000 to 11,500 feet in elevation; dominated by rocks, hardy wildflowers, grasses, lichens and scattered low shrubs.

Alternate attachment: An arrangement of leaves in which individual leaves are attached to the stem in an alternating pattern, with some distance between each leaf. (*Compare:* Opposite attachment, Whorled attachment)

Annual: A plant which lives for one season only; reproduction is by seed rather than from roots. (*Compare:* Perennial)

Anther: The pollen-producing element of a flower.

Areole: A rounded, tuft-like bud on a cactus from which spines (and, in some species, glochids) typically grow.

Basal: Leaves growing at the base of a plant, often in a whorl or rosette.

Berry: A simple, fleshy fruit containing one or more carpels, each with one or more seeds; the seeds are relatively soft. (*Compare:* Capsule, Cone, Drupe, Pepo, Pome, Pseudocarp)

Blade: The entire grouping of leaflets, stemlets and central leaf stalk that makes up a compound leaf. The word "blade" is also used to describe the wide, flat part of a simple leaf.

Bloom: A light-colored or waxy coating on a fruit or stem that gives it a dusty appearance.

Bract: A petal-like structure at the base of a flower.

Bramble: A sprawling, vine-like shrub with arching branches that are often thorny or prickly.

Cane: A flexible, woody stem; usually used to describe brambles such as raspberries.

Capsule: A dry, non-fleshy fruit that splits at maturity to scatter seeds. (*Compare:* Berry, Cone, Drupe, Pepo, Pome, Pseudocarp)

Carpel: Part of the ovary of a plant, containing ovules (eggs).

Cathartic: Purgative; causing diarrhea or vomiting.

Catkin: A spike-like structure with tiny unisexual flowers, often having a fuzzy appearance.

Clasping: A leaf that attaches directly to the stem, with no leaf stalk; the base of the leaf clasps, or slightly surrounds, the stem but does not extend beyond it. (*Compare:* Peltate, Perfoliate, Sessile)

Cleft: A linear depression with smooth edges.

Compound drupe: A fleshy fruit formed from a single flower but composed of many drupes, each containing one seed; synonymous with aggregate drupe.

Compound leaf: A leaf composed of a central leaf stalk with two or more leaflets. A compound leaf has a bud at its base; a leaflet does not. (*Compare:* Simple leaf)

Cone: A fruit consisting of scales arranged in an overlapping or spiral fashion around a central core; seeds develop between the scales. (*Compare:* Berry, Capsule, Drupe, Pepo, Pome, Pseudocarp)

Coniferous: A tree with needle-like or scale-like leaves (usually evergreen) whose seeds are contained in cones. (*Compare:* Hardwood)

Crown: A remnant of the flower, found on the base of some fruits; it looks like a circle of pointed, dried leaf tips. Also used to refer to the top of a tree or shrub, particularly one with a rounded appearance.

Cyme: A flat-topped cluster of flowers or fruits.

Dappled: A forested area that receives sunlight broken up by light leaf cover.

Deciduous: A tree or shrub whose leaves fall off at the end of the growing season. (*Compare:* Evergreen)

Dehiscent: A fruit that dries out and splits open to release its seeds; legumes are dehiscent. (*Compare:* Indehiscent)

Doubly compound leaf: A compound leaf consisting of two or more compound blades attached to the central leaf stalk. Only the main leaf stalk has a bud at the base; the secondary compound leaves are not true leaves and have no bud.

Doubly toothed leaf: Each leaf tooth has one or more smaller teeth, making for a jagged edge that alternates between coarse and fine teeth.

Downy: Having fine, soft hairs.

Drupe: A simple, fleshy fruit with a hard pit (stone); the pit typically contains one seed but can contain more. (*Compare:* Berry, Capsule, Compound drupe, Cone, Pepo, Pome, Pseudocarp)

Elliptic: A leaf that is roughly oval in shape; ends may be pointed or rounded.

Endangered: A native plant whose populations have been depleted by animal predation or over-harvesting, or whose growing area has been reduced by pollution, habitat loss or over-competition from other plants.

Evergreen: Leaves that remain green year round; also used to refer to a tree containing evergreen leaves. (*Compare:* Deciduous)

Filament: A long stalk that holds the anther, the pollen-producing part of a plant.

Flower stalk: A separate stem that carries the flowers but no leaves; synonymous with fruiting stalk.

Follicle: A dry fruit derived from a single carpel; follicles dry out and split open on one side only to release their seeds. (*Compare:* Legume, Nut)

Foothills zone: The transition zone between the plains and the true mountains; generally from 5,000 to 8,000 feet in elevation.

Fruit: The ripened part of a plant that disperses seeds. (*See* Berry, Capsule, Cone, Drupe, Pepo, Pome, Pseudocarp)

Fruiting stalk: A separate stem that carries the fruits but no leaves; synonymous with flowering stalk.

Genus: A category used in taxonomy to describe a group of related plants; a rank below family but above species.

Gland: A cell, small organ or structure that secretes (discharges) minute amounts of fluids or other substances.

Glochid: Sharp, tiny barbed bristles that grow from the areole on *Opuntia* and *Cylindropuntia* cactus species; glochids are so fine that they may seem invisible.

Grasslands: Semi-arid areas dominated by perennial grasses and scattered low shrubs.

Hardwood: A broad-leaved tree whose seeds are contained in fruits or nuts. (*Compare:* Coniferous)

High-desert plateau: Dry, hot area characterized by scrubby, drought-tolerant shrubs; generally from 5,000 to 8,000 feet in elevation.

Indehiscent: A fruit that dries out but does not split open; nuts are indehiscent. (*Compare:* Dehiscent)

Introduced: A plant, often from Europe or Asia, that did not grow naturally in the wild in our area but was planted as an ornamental or a food crop; sometimes planted to control erosion or provide shade. Synonymous with non-native.

Invasive: A plant, generally non-native, that spreads rapidly and crowds out native plants, shades understory plants, or depletes soil of moisture.

Krummholz: Shrubs and trees that have been twisted by fierce winds into shortened, gnarled shapes; generally found near or above the treeline.

Lance-shaped: A leaf that is long and slender, with sides that are almost parallel for much of the length.

Leaf axil: The point at which a leaf stalk (from a simple or compound leaf) joins the stem; synonymous with leaf node.

Leaflet: An individual leaf-like member of a compound leaf. A leaflet does not have a bud at its base; only true leaves such as the compound leaf and the simple leaf have a bud at the base.

Leaf node: The point at which a leaf stalk (from a simple or compound leaf) joins the stem; synonymous with leaf axil.

Legume: A pod containing pea-like seeds; legumes dry out and split open to release their seeds. (*Compare:* Follicle, Nut)

Lenticel: A breathing pore, appearing as a bump or raised line in the bark of a tree or woody shrub.

Lobed leaf: A leaf that has several distinct sections, typically scalloped or pointed.

Midrib: The central rib of a leaf.

Mixed-wood forest: A forest having both hardwood and coniferous trees.

Montane zone: The lower mountains, typically from 8,000 to 9,500 feet; in this zone, vegetation gradually changes from scrub to tall forests.

Multiple fruit: A single fruit formed from multiple flowers that grow together in a cluster.

Mycoheterotrophy: A relationship in which a non-chlorophyll-producing plant gets its nutrients from fungi that, in turn, survive by extracting nutrients from trees and other plants.

Node: A joining point between a leaf stem and the main stem or between two stems.

Non-native: A plant, often from Europe or Asia, that did not grow naturally in the wild in our area but was planted as an ornamental or a food crop; sometimes planted to control erosion or provide shade. Synonymous with introduced.

Nut: A large, dry fruit with a hard seedcoat, usually containing a single seed; nuts are indehiscent. (*Compare:* Follicle, Legume)

Opposite attachment: An arrangement of leaves in which individual leaves are attached to the stem directly across from one another. (*Compare:* Alternate attachment, Whorled attachment)

Ovary: A case containing carpels, which hold the ovules (eggs); a component of the pistil.

Paddle-shaped: A leaf whose shape resembles that of a canoe paddle: narrow at the base, widening at or above the midpoint with a broad tip that is typically rounded.

Palmately compound: An arrangement of leaflets in a compound leaf in which individual leaflets radiate from a central point, similar to fingers radiating from the palm of a hand. (*Compare:* Pinnately compound)

Pectin: A natural thickening agent found in apples and some other fruits; pectin helps jelly and jam "set" or thicken naturally.

Peltate: A leaf whose stem is attached on the underside, slightly away from the base of the leaf. (*Compare:* Clasping, Perfoliate, Sessile)

Pepo: A simple fruit with a tough rind developed from the receptacle. (*Compare:* Berry, Capsule, Cone, Drupe, Pome, Pseudocarp)

Perennial: A plant whose greenery, flowers and fruit die back each season but that grows again the following year from the same root. (*Compare:* Annual)

Perfoliate: A leaf whose base extends slightly beyond the stem, giving the impression that the stem is growing up through the leaf. (*Compare:* Clasping, Peltate, Sessile)

Petiole: The stemlet that attaches a leaf, or a leaflet, to the stem or leaf stalk.

Photosynthesis: The process by which a plant converts sunlight to food.

Pinnately compound: An arrangement of leaflets in a compound leaf in which individual leaflets are arranged either alternately or oppositely along the central leaf stalk. (*Compare:* Palmately compound)

Pistil: The female part of a flower, consisting of an ovary, style and stigma; usually in the center of the flower.

Plains zone: A habitat zone that is below 5,000 feet in elevation.

Pome: A simple fruit whose flesh is developed from the receptacle. (*Compare:* Berry, Capsule, Cone, Drupe, Pepo, Pseudocarp)

Pseudocarp: A simple fruit, such as a pome or pepo, whose flesh is developed from a part other than the ovary. (*Compare:* Berry, Capsule, Cone, Drupe, Pepo, Pome)

Raceme: A long cluster of multiple flowers, each growing on a stemlet that is attached to a central stalk; stemlets are equal in length. Sometimes used to refer to the arrangement of fruits which follow the flowers. (*Compare:* Umbrella-like cluster)

Racemose: Like a raceme; sometimes used to refer to the arrangement of the fruits which follow flowers growing in a raceme.

Receptacle: An enlarged area at the base of a flower, just below the reproductive structures. In compound drupes, the receptacle is the core of the fruit.

Rhizome: An underground stem that produces lateral shoots and roots at intervals.

Riparian: Areas along creeks, lakes and rivers.

Runner: A shoot growing from the base of a shrub, capable of rooting along its length.

Semi-desert shrubland zone: Dry, hot area characterized by scrubby, drought-tolerant shrubs; generally from 5,000 to 8,000 feet in elevation.

Sepal: A type of petal in the outermost group at the base of a flower; typically green and leaf-like.

Serrated: Finely toothed.

Sessile: A leaf that attaches directly to the stem, with no leaf stalk. (*Compare:* Clasping, Peltate, Perfoliate)

Simple leaf: A single, true leaf with a bud at the base of the leaf stem. (*Compare:* Compound leaf, Leaflet)

Sinus: The depression between lobes of a leaf.

Spadix: A club-like structure with many small flowers (later, fruits) clustered tightly together on a spike; usually partially enclosed by a spathe.

Spathe: A large petal-like structure, sometimes curled into a tube-like shape, which partially surrounds a flowering cluster called a spadix.

Stamen: The male part of a flower, consisting of the anther and filament; usually around the edges of the inside of a flower.

Stemlet: A secondary stem that connects a flower, fruit or leaflet to the main stem.

Stem succulent: A non-woody plant such as cactus that holds water in its soft tissue.

Stigma: The part of a flower that collects and germinates pollen, which it then sends down the style into the ovules contained in the ovary.

Style: A long stalk that holds the stigma, which is the pollen-gathering part of a plant.

Sub-alpine zone: Middle mountain elevations, from about 9,500 feet to the treeline, characterized by harsh climate and short growing season; mostly coniferous trees.

Subshrub: A perennial with a woody base and non-woody stems.

Sucker: A shoot that grows from the underground roots at the base of a plant; suckering plants often form thickets.

Talus: An area of broken rock at the base of a cliff or hill; also called *scree*.

Tendril: A thread-like appendage, found on climbing vines, that coils around other plants or objects.

Terminal leaflet: The leaflet at the end of a compound leaf that has an uneven numbers of leaflets; the other leaflets are paired.

Thicket: A dense cluster of shrubs, trees or brushy plants.

Toothed leaf: A leaf with multiple points (teeth) around the edge. Teeth can be sharply pointed or rounded. *See also* Doubly toothed leaf.

Treeline: The area above which large trees can no longer grow, generally above 10,000 to 11,500 feet in elevation.

Trifoliate leaf: A compound leaf with three leaflets.

True leaf: A simple leaf, or a compound leaf, with a bud at the base. (*Compare:* Leaflet)

Tuber: A thickened portion of an underground stem, containing buds from which new growth will sprout; the common potato is a well-known tuber.

Tubercle: A rounded, pillowy bump or knob-like projection on a cactus.

Umbrella-like cluster: A cluster of multiple flowers (or the fruits which follow the flowers), each growing on a stemlet that is attached to a single point on the central stalk. If stemlets are equal in length, the cluster is rounded; if stalks are varying in length (or branched into shorter stalks), the cluster has a flat top. (*Compare:* Raceme)

Whorled attachment: An arrangement of leaves in which three or more leaves attach to a central point. (*Compare:* Alternate attachment, Opposite attachment)

INDEX

ABOUT THE AUTHOR

Teresa Marrone has been gathering and preparing wild edibles for more than 20 years. She was formerly Managing Editor of a series of outdoors-themed books, and is the author of *Abundantly Wild: Collecting and Cooking Wild Edibles in the Upper Midwest*, as well as numerous other outdoors-related cookbooks. Teresa has also written many magazine articles on wild foods and cooking, and has recently re-kindled an early interest in photography.

Wild Berries & Fruits Field Guide of the Rocky Mountain States combines her various skills and interests into a clear, concise, easy-to-use book that helps the user appreciate the diversity of the various wild berries and other fruits that grow in this region. Teresa lives in Minneapolis with husband Bruce and their Senegal parrot, Tuca.